Dearly beloved

A biography of John and Dorothy French

Winston C. Fraser

© 2020 Winston Fraser Consulting Inc.

1225 rue Bellevue
Saint-Lazare, QC J7T 2L9
438-969-2510
wcfraser@sympatico.ca

All rights reserved. No part of this book may be adapted, reproduced or transmitted in any form or by any means, electronic, mechanical, photocopying, recording, microrecording, or otherwise, without the written permission of Winston Fraser Consulting, Inc.

Layout and production: Jim Fraser

Front cover photo: Malcolm Fraser collection

Back cover photos:
    Top left: courtesy of Mary Watson
    Top middle: courtesy of Alice Wickenden MacEwen
    Top right: Malcolm Fraser collection
    Author: Carol Rand

Printed and bound in Canada by:
Katari Imaging
282 Elgin St.
Ottawa, ON K2P 1M3
613-233-1999
www.katariimaging.com

Printed and bound in the USA by:
Ingram Spark (www.ingramspark.com) and others

ISBN: 978-1-7771308-5-5

Dedication

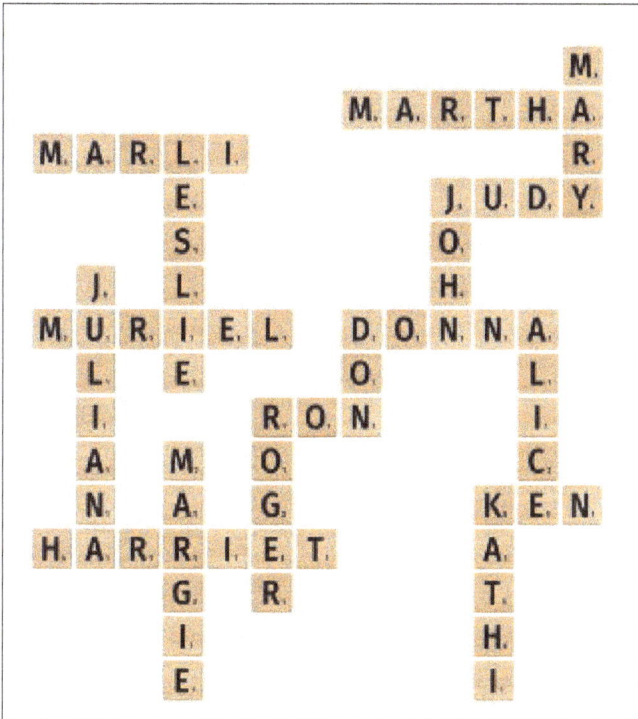

French and MacLeod family contributors
(thepuzzleposter.com)

This book is gratefully dedicated to John and Dorothy French's nieces, nephews, grandnieces, grandnephews and cousins, whose contributions and cooperation made the creation of this book possible. Their generous sharing of family historical information, personal memories, photographs and other memorabilia was invaluable.

A simple "thank you" seems so inadequate. So, to each and every one of you, let me also say *merci beaucoup* and *gratias tibi valde*. Or to borrow a quotation from Shakespeare's *Twelfth Night*,

> "I can no other answer make but thanks,
> And thanks, and ever thanks."

Foreword

Studying history to most of us means studying history on a grand scale. The rise and fall of civilizations, the progress of major social and economic changes, everything in short that affects whole countries, peoples and world events. The big picture of history as given by these studies is vitally important, but it is worthwhile to remember that those major processes and events we learn about were made up of individuals, families, locales and communities that all played their part in shaping and being shaped by history. – *University of Toronto*

For many of us, our first prolonged exposure to "history" occurs in high school. Sadly, the subject can seem dry, even boring, to many students. That perception is often the result of school curricula, which tend to emphasize political leaders, major national events and important dates. The resulting lack of interest in all things historical can be lifelong.

Many organizations advocate for the inclusion of "local history" in school programming. The idea is that the events that shaped our towns and villages and neighbourhoods, and the people who lived and worked in them, can be infinitely more relatable to people, regardless of age, than history as told "on a grand scale." Or, as the Quebec Anglophone Heritage Network put it in its 2016 recommendation to Quebec's Ministry of Education, the inclusion of local history in the teaching curriculum would "accommodate local historical issues, such as shipbuilding in the Gaspé, agricultural settlement in the Eastern Townships, or the lumber industry in the Laurentians," and "enhance the need for students to see themselves and their communities reflected in the wider history of Quebec and Canada."

In other words, learning about the movers and shakers in one's own community, about how a town got its name, or about the people who lived in the oldest home on the street (maybe our grandparents knew them!), can be the easiest way to pique someone's interest in history. Additionally, if people can be interested in history at a community level, they are more likely to develop an interest in history on that grand scale. Whether it is politics, economics, or everyday human interaction, local history is truly a microcosm for society at large.

Bringing local history to life, it should be said, is not just the purview of schools, teachers and curricula. It is also the job of museums, historical societies and, of course, historians.

The present book, *Dearly beloved*, by local historian Winston C. Fraser, is a case in point. In this book, as with others Mr. Fraser has written, notably *Dew Drop Inn: Lasting Memories of a Cookshire Landmark* (2017), the author demonstrates an ability to weave together anecdotes and lore to create a captivating account of the subject matter. Mr. Fraser's enthusiasm for the story comes through in every page.

Like the author's previous books, *Dearly beloved*, which focuses on the life and times of John and Dorothy French, the author's Cookshire godparents, relies heavily on personal memories, family history, local newspaper accounts, and a rich mine of memorabilia to tell the story not only of a "beloved" local couple, but also the community in which they lived. *Dearly beloved*, which is lavishly illustrated with selections from the family archives, is a fine contribution to the ever-growing body of work on local Eastern Townships history.

– Matthew Farfan, Stanstead, Que.

Preface

The idea for this book was conceived shortly after the passing of my older brother Malcolm in March 2020. While looking through his copious collection of Cookshire historical memorabilia, I came across a beautiful framed photograph of our godparents, John and Dorothy French, who had both passed away 50 years ago, in 1970. At that moment, I was reminded of what a well-respected Cookshire couple they were, and so decided they deserved to have a book written about them.

But there was one big problem: I realized I knew very little about them. Basically, I knew them as a friendly older couple who paid generously for occasional odd jobs my siblings and I did for them. I needed to know much more, so I placed an ad in *The [Sherbrooke] Record* to invite its readers to share their memories of the Frenches. The result was a giant goose-egg. Then I polled my siblings for **their** recollections. Although they responded with several interesting anecdotes, I still did not have nearly enough material to justify a book.

Finally, I turned to the Internet – today's fountain of all knowledge – where I discovered a website that contained detailed genealogical information about the French family. I contacted its creator, Ken Watson (a grandnephew of John and Dorothy), who immediately sounded the clarion call to other members of the extended French family. They, in turn, generously responded with a flood of memories and memorabilia. As a result, I began to really **know** my godparents. Among the surprising facts I learned as I pursued this project were the following:

- John French was not the serious, reserved man I had imagined – in fact, to his family he was quite the opposite.
- Dorothy French was much more than the petite lady with the perpetual smile I remember – she was a talented teacher, a businesswoman, and a leadership giant in the community.
- Neither John nor Dorothy were natives of Cookshire, even though they lived there for their entire married life.
- They were married in a very private ceremony in a very exotic place – New York City.
- Although I always knew my godfather as being dressed in a suit and tie, he much earlier was a farmer who would later be called upon to act as a swine midwife (or should I say "mid-husband!") at my dad's farm.

- After the passing of their respective fathers, John and Dorothy each cared several years for their widowed mothers.
- I was aware that John had been a Member of Quebec's Legislative Assembly (MLA), but little did I realize he had been a long-time political junkie who only reluctantly became a politician per se.
- I had no idea that Dorothy was a Macdonald College-educated teacher who began her teaching career in a one-room rural schoolhouse before moving to one of the largest elementary schools in Montreal, where she witnessed an unprecedented students' strike.
- In spite of having no children of their own, John and Dorothy related remarkably well to children and young people.
- Although I appreciated my godparents' remuneration for occasional tasks my siblings and I did for them, I was unaware of the extent of their generosity, in terms of both their time and their treasure, to so many organizations and individuals.
- John was affected all his life by a medical condition inherited from his father that would be passed on to later generations.

As a child and teenager growing up in Cookshire, I only knew of a few of John's many siblings. Now, thanks to information provided by his siblings' children and grandchildren, I feel like I know them all, having learned of their own unique life stories.

In the chapters that follow, you will read about all this and more, because this book is not only a biography of my godparents. It is also a history of their adventurous ancestors, a salute to their several siblings, a description of their Cookshire homes, a portrait of their nearby neighbours, and a light-hearted look at their final resting place. But, above all, it is a tribute to a dearly beloved couple.

Acknowledgements

Firstly, I wish to acknowledge the members of John and Dorothy French's families, whose kind collaborations made this book possible. In addition, I want to recognize the contributions of my own family members and friends who so kindly shared their memories or assisted in any other way. The list is long and I apologize in advance to anyone who may have been inadvertently omitted. To all of the following I extend my sincere thanks:

Alice Wickenden MacEwen, Allan Rowell, Almon Pope, Barbara Roskell, Ben Hodge, Bill Lawson, Bruce Learned, Carl Jackson, Charles W. K. Fraser, Clyne Macdonald, David Fraser, David Laberee, Derek Booth, Diane Fraser Keet, Don French, Donna Mikulecky, Doris Pope, Dorothy Ross, Erwin Watson, Evelyn Yvonne Theriault, Frasier Bellam, Fred Hurd, Gilles Denis, Harriet Wickenden Taylor, Jack Garneau, Janice Fraser, Jayne Shrimpton, Jean-François Nadeau, Jim Fraser, Jim Hurd, Jody Robinson, Joel Barter, John "Jack" Fraser, John French Wickenden, John Mackley, Judy Moorey, Juliana French, June Fraser Patterson, Karen Fraser Jackson, Kathi Kressman, Ken Watson, Kerri Fraser, Larry Diamond, Leslie Buckle, Leslie Nutbrown, Linda Hoy, Mac Learned, Magz Macleod, Margie French, Marilyn Fraser Reed, Marli Mikulecky, Martha Wickenden MacKellar, Mary Anne Poutanen, Mary Watson, Matthew Farfan, Muriel French Fitzsimmons, Muriel Watson, Neil Burns, Perry Beaton, Rachel Garber, Robert Burns, Roderick MacLeod, Rodger Heatherington, Roger Lancey, Ron Buckle, Sally Harmer, Serena Wintle, Sharon Moore, Sharron Hodge Rothney, Stanley Parker, Steve Fraser, Warren Fraser.

I would be remiss to not mention the valuable information contained in the daily diaries kept by my late grandmother, Lilla Joyce Fraser, my late mother, Alice Hood Fraser, my late cousin Mabel Fraser McVetty, and my late wife, Becky Humphrey Fraser. Appreciation is extended to my brother Warren for his detailed analysis of our mother's diaries to enable selection of pertinent information. I also want to thank artist James Harvey for his excellent cartoon sketches and Greg Beck for his professional photo retouching. Finally, a special word of appreciation to my brother Jim for his expert proofreading, layout and production services.

Contents

Dedication		3
Foreword		5
Preface		7
Acknowledgements		9
Chapter 1	The Frenches: From Connecticut to Compton County	13
Chapter 2	The MacLeods: From Lewis to Lingwick	31
Chapter 3	John: A Man of Many Hats	41
Chapter 4	Dorothy: A Woman with Class	57
Chapter 5	Love and Marriage	69
Chapter 6	Uncle John and Aunt Dorothy	77
Chapter 7	John W. French, MLA	95
Chapter 8	Retirement Living: A Life of Giving	109
Chapter 9	Salute to Siblings	121
Chapter 10	A Special Kind of Family	153
Chapter 11	Cookshire Homes on Main and Craig	163
Chapter 12	Nearby Neighbours	175
Chapter 13	Resting in Peace "Up on the Hill"	185
Epilogue		193
Appendix: Ancestral Obituaries Scrapbook		195

Chapter 1
The Frenches: From Connecticut to Compton County

It is indeed a desirable thing to be well-descended, but the glory belongs to our ancestors. – Plutarch

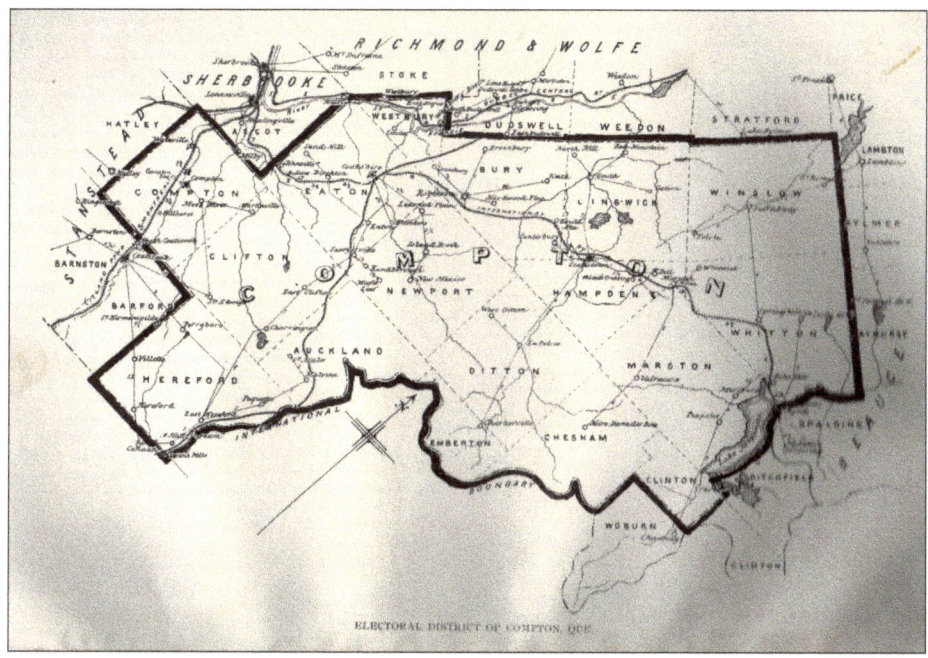

1896 map of Compton County (*History of Compton County*)

This first two chapters of this book pay homage to the ancestors of John French and Dorothy MacLeod, both of whose forebears were pioneers in the white colonization of the "wastelands" of Compton County in the Eastern Townships of what was then Lower Canada. It is important to recognize that the land on which they settled is part of the unceded territories of the Abenaki First Nations peoples who had frequented the area for many centuries prior as their seasonal hunting and fishing grounds.

In this chapter we look at the origin of the French surname, explore the family's English roots and provide in-depth portrayals of John French's Compton County ancestors.

The French surname

There are many different theories about the origin of the French family name. Here is one of them:

The surname French was originally "de Freynes" and was originally derived from the Latin word "fraxinus," which means an "ash tree." This surname was first found in Devon [England]. They were descendants of Theophilus de France who accompanied William the Conqueror into England in 1066. . . . A crest associated with the French family contains the motto "*Malo mori quam foedari*" ("Death rather than disgrace"). (reference: houseofnames.com)

Compton County Museum, Eaton (photo by author)

Explaining to someone that your name is actually "French" can sometimes lead to interesting conversations, as illustrated in this anecdote described by one of John's nieces:

> Former Globe and Mail Literary Editor, William French, once wrote a column about his surname and the difficulties it could present, to wit, making a reservation. "Your name, sir?" "It's French." "That's all right, sir, go ahead." "No, I mean it's French." "That's all right, sir, go ahead." And so on. (Alice Wickenden MacEwen)

The French family origins

John's grandnephew Ken Watson has traced the French family's origins back to England, where Jacob French was born in 1553 near Assington, Suffolk. The French Family Association website lists a total of almost 6000 Jacob French descendants, spanning some 11 generations. (references: rideau-info.com; frenchfamilyassoc.com)

In this biography, we will limit ourselves to John French's latest three generations of ancestors as indicated in the pedigree chart on the opposite page.

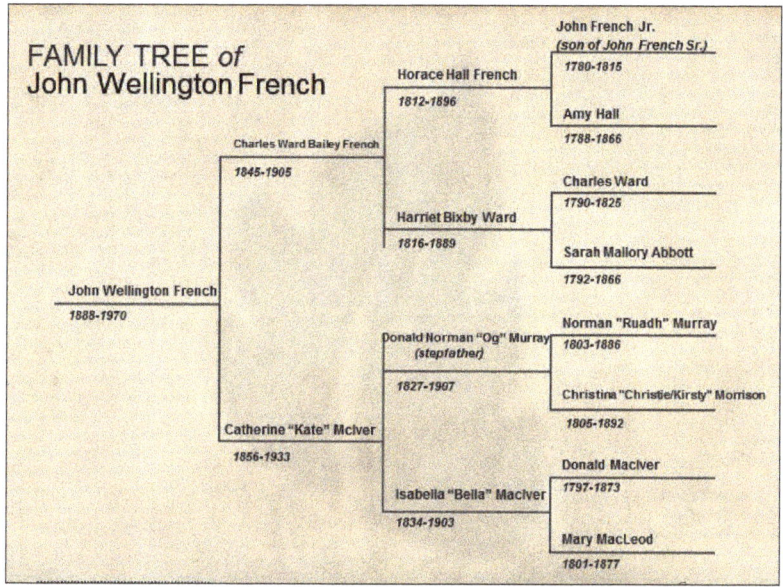

John W. French family tree pedigree chart (genealogybank.com)

John's great-grandfather John French

John's great-grandfather (also named John French) was, with **his** father John (John French Sr.) and his brothers Levi and Luther, among the first white settlers of Compton County, arriving in Eaton Township in 1796. The Frenches' trek north from New Hampshire – although they were born in Enfield, Connecticut – was the direct result of a milestone Canadian political event.

In 1791 the Constitutional Act was passed – an Act of the British Parliament creating Upper Canada and Lower Canada and opening the Eastern Townships "waste lands" to settlement. Excerpts from the Act and the Royal Proclamation of 1792 follow:

> CONSTITUTIONAL ACT AND INSTRUCTIONS OF 1791: XLIII. All lands which shall be hereafter granted . . . in free and common soccage [i.e. the Crown no longer holds title to the land] . . . , in like manner as lands are now holden in free and common soccage [i.e., the Crown no longer holds title to the land] . . . within the said Province of Lower Canada . . . (swquebec.ca)

> A PROCLAMATION To such as are desirous to settle on the Lands of the Crown in the Province of Lower Canada: By His Excellency ALURED CLARKE, Esquire, Lieutenant Governor and Commander in Chief of the said Province, and Major General of His Majesty's Forces, etc. BE IT KNOWN to all concerned . . . the Terms of Grant and Settlement. . . (eco.canadiana.ca)

Dearly beloved

List of the Leader and Associates proposed for the Township of Eaton in the Province of Lower Canada.

	1	Josiah Sawyer Leader		Lower Canada
17 mch 96	2	Jabez Baldwin		of New Hampshire
Do	3	Nathan Baldwin		Do ... Do
	4	John Perry		Do ... Do
17 mch 96	5	Abner Osgood		Do ... Do
	6	Philip Jordan		Do ... Do
21 mch 96	7	John Jordan		Do ... Do
Do	8	Benjamin Bishop		Do ... Do
	9	Royal Larned		Do ... Do
	10	Job Hugh		Do ... Do
	11	William Jordan		Do ... Do
	12	William McAlister		Do ... Do
3 M 96	13	Abel Bennet		Do ... Do
21 mch 96	14	James Luther		Do ... Do
	15	John French	←	Do ... Do
5 feb 1796	16	Levi French		Do ... Do
July 96	17	Abner Powers		Do ... Do
5 feb 1796	18	Luther French		
	19	James Lucas		State Vermont
	20	Samuel Beach		Do ... Do
	21	Orsamus Bailey		Do ... Do
	22	Ward Bailey Junr		Do ... Do
	23	Isaac Stephens		Do ... Do
	24	Samuel Hugh		Do ... Do
	25	Moses Hugh		Do ... Do
	26	William Cutler		Do ... Do
	27	Royal Cutler		Do ... Do
	28	Israel Bailey		Do ... Do
	29	John Cook		Do ... Do
	30	Amos Hawley		Do ... Do
	31	Charles Cutler		Do ... Do
14 feb 96	32	Timothy Bailey		Do ... Do
	33	Christopher L. Bailey		Do ... Do
	34	Thomas Beach		State Connecticut
July 96	35	Jesse Cooper		Do ... Do
	36	Edmund Heard		State Massachusetts
	37	Jesse Hugh		State Vermont

Josiah Sawyer land grant: partial list of Associates, including John French Sr. (bac-lac.gc.ca)

The Josiah Sawyer connection

This above-mentioned Proclamation provided the impetus for the Frenches' migration to Canada. However, were it not for the initiative of a man named Josiah Sawyer, they might never have ended up in Canada as pioneers of Eaton Township. Sawyer, a former military man who served in the American War of Independence, was the "Leader" of a group of "Associates" wanting to take advantage of the government's offer of free land. John French Sr. (as well as John Jr.'s brothers Levi and Luther) were members of that company of Associates. John French Jr. would follow shortly thereafter.

Sawyer's remarkable efforts to secure the Township of Eaton for himself and his Associates are well-documented:

> Captain Josiah Sawyer, from whom the village of Sawyerville takes its name, was in all likelihood the first settler in Eaton.... In the year 1793 [he] set out from Missiskoui (sic) Bay, on Lake Champlain, with provisions, tools, etc., through the woods, ninety miles from any inhabitants to the westward, and after traveling and exploring the woods thirty-one days arrived . . . in Newport where he . . . began to make improvements, distant twenty-five miles from any inhabitants to the south and seventy miles from the French settlements to the north. (L.S. Channell, *History of Compton County*, 1896)

Sawyer's indefatigable efforts to obtain a land grant continued for almost 10 years. The first step was to prepare a formal application called a Memorial (the person preparing the application is referred to as the Memorialist). Below is an excerpt from Sawyer's Memorial dated July 23, 1793. As the reader will note, he goes to great lengths to excuse his service in the war against Great Britain and to profess his new-found allegiance to the King.

> That in the commencement of the troubles in America your Memorialist being then of the age of nineteen years & before the Declaration of Independence was made by the Americans. He was appointed an officer in the American Army, but that upon the Declaration of Independence as soon as he could possibly leave the Service he resigned his Commission & from principle refused to take arms against Great Britain, that this resolution drew on him the displeasure of the Committees & subjected him to be frequently harassed by them. But that he rigidly notwithstanding their oppression, continued to persevere in that resolution to the End of the war . . . That your Memorialist from an attachment to the King's Government, availed himself of the first opportunity of moving into this Province, that he might live under it, for which purpose he came into this Province & settled at Mississquoi Bay in the year 1787 where he has continued to reside since . . . (Josiah Sawyer Papers, bac-lac.gc.ca)

Among the prerequisites for a land grant was that the Leader had to submit the names of his Associates and have each of them take the Oath and declare their allegiance as indicated below. John French Sr. took the Oath on October 13, 1795.

> OATH OF ALLEGIANCE: "I, John French, do sincerely promise and swear, that I will be faithful and bear true Allegiance to His Majesty King George; so help me God."

> DECLARATION: "I, John French, do promise and declare that I will maintain and defend to the utmost of my Power the Authority of the King in His Parliament as the supreme Legislature of this Province" (Toronto Public Library)

The Leader also had to pay the costs to survey his desired Township. In Sawyer's case, it amounted to 15 pounds. Another requirement for the Leader was to vouch (in writing) for the character of each of his Associates:

> I declare that I am personally acquainted with the following person [John French and the other Associates] all of whom I can recommend as good character; such as I am fully of the opinion will make good Subjects and useful settlers in the Province of Lower Canada. (Josiah Sawyer Papers, bac-lac.gc.ca)

In a final report to secure the letters patent for his land grant, Sawyer proudly summarized what he had done to earn it:

> The persevering indefatigable industry and assiduity of Mr. Sawyer . . . with unabating labour, suffering great hardships (for the first two years) has he together with his Associates been able in the course of six years to cut out in the middle of a wilderness an extensive flourishing settlement . . . [referring to John French specifically] Log house, a large frame barn. He resides on the lot with a numerous family. (Josiah Sawyer Papers, bac-lac.gc.ca)

Finally, in 1800 Sawyer is able to formally grant 1200 acres of lots to John French Sr. and to the other Associates who had met the requirements of clearing several acres and establishing a homestead. Among John's lots was Lot 9 of Range 9, which today represents a large portion of the Town of Cookshire.

In the early years of the Eaton settlement, the colonists were occasionally visited by a travelling merchant from Attleborough, Massachusetts. Each family or individual had a page in the salesman's account book. John French Jr.'s entry is reproduced opposite.

Without a road network, the new settlers faced enormous challenges in terms of the transportation of goods, as described in L.S. Channell's *History of Compton County*:

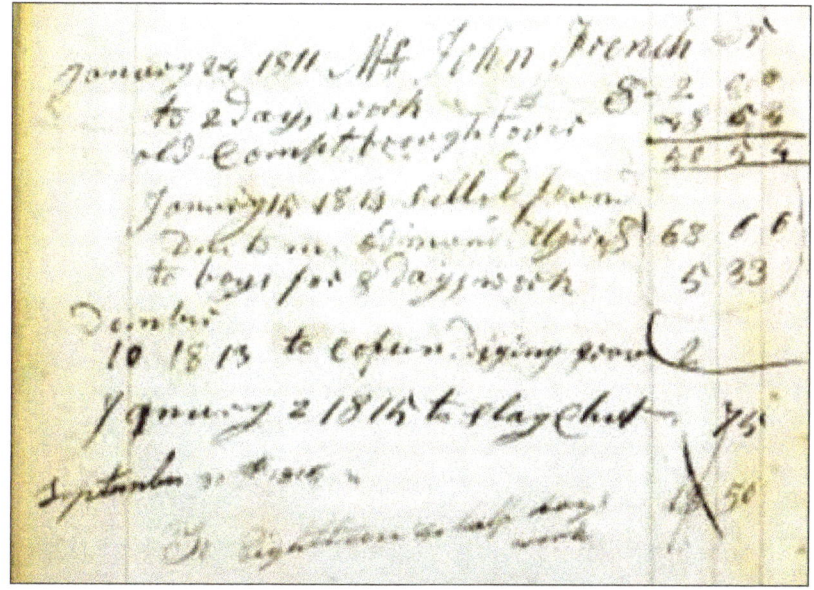

Josiah Sawyer land grant distribution to Associates, including John French (red borders), 1800 (numerique.banq.qc.ca)

John French Jr.'s Attleborough account book page, 1811-1815 (numerique.banq.qc.ca)

Dearly beloved

Up to the time of the building of the Grand Trunk Railway, all marketing was done either by boat or team to Three Rivers or Montreal. The Eaton and St. Francis rivers gave the settlers good transportation for those days . . . The boats were sent down the St. Francis river to its junction with the St. Lawrence, and there, produce was transferred to larger boats for Montreal, Quebec, Three Rivers and other places. The principal article exported in those days was pearl-ash, made from hardwood ashes. This sold for about $12. per one hundred pounds. Flour and other necessaries were bought back in exchange. These journeys by boat were always dangerous, and necessitated hard labour at places like Brompton Falls, where everything had to be [unloaded and] carried around on land in both directions. (*History of Compton County*)

Tragedy strikes

Tragically, one such journey claimed the life of John French Jr. at the young age of 35 years. This very sad event was recounted in an article written by John's cousin, Hiram French, in 1891:

These boating trips were sometimes attended with much danger. One [such] instance I will mention. In the month of May, 1815, some parties wished to market their products and prepared for the river trip. Among those who went were John Lebourveau, as captain, John French Jr., D.W. Rogers, and others and Captain Samuel Heard of Newport [Township], who with his family, were starting for Upper Canada. His family had

Shooting the falls at Brompton (sketch by James Harvey)

preceded him to a point below Great Brompton Falls, a few miles below Sherbrooke, but Heard said he would like to go and help run the boat over the Falls. This was on the 25th of May, 1815. There was plenty of help to take the boat over the falls, but the river was uncommonly high, much higher than the men expected to find it. The loading had been taken by [horse] teams to below the Falls.

They started down the Falls but found the river so high that they could not manage the boat. In the middle of the Falls, they struck the shore, and all jumped out, but as the hind end of the boat came around, John French, who was a stout resolute man, got in and said "Men, if we want to save the boat, now is the time." Captain Heard caught the warp on the bow end of the boat to help save it, but the others were frightened, and said it was of no use, and as the boat swung around, it pulled Heard in after it. The lower side of the boat struck a rock, and immediately capsized, throwing French underneath. He soon came to the surface, and being a good swimmer, put to the opposite shore, but as he went out of the swift water into the eddy, he sank. Captain Heard was also a good swimmer, and appeared to be unhurt as he swam down the river. It seemed as though he would succeed in reaching the other shore. One of the men from the shore said to him "Don't be frightened" and he sank to rise no more.

The news of this sad accident cast a gloom all over this section of the Eastern Townships, and was a blow to the respective families of the deceased. The loss of those men was felt to be a public loss as well. French lived in what is now Cookshire, and there never was a man who lived there who was more missed than he was. (*Sherbrooke Daily Record*, Mar. 16, 1957; reprinted from *The Land We Live In*, 1891)

John's grandfather Horace Hall French

Horace Hall French and Harriet French in 1851 Census of Eaton (ancestry.ca)

John Wellington French's grandfather, Horace Hall French, was born on the old Hurd farm at Cookshire, in 1812, just three years before the untimely passing of his father, John, described above. Although he was initially a farmer, Horace was best known as an innkeeper, first in Cookshire, then later in Scotstown.

L.S. Channell provides details of Horace's impressive entrepreneurial accomplishments:

> Mr. H. H. French built the hotel in Cookshire, now owned by A. Learned, also the store now owned and occupied by S. J. Osgood, and later the hotel at Scotstown, now owned by his son.

> Alden Learned, proprietor of the Cookshire House, . . . purchased his present hotel from Mr. H. H. French, now of Scotstown, who had erected the building in 1850. Previous to Mr. Learned's purchase, the place had been carried on by Mr. H. H. French.

> The first hotel [in Scotstown] was built about the time of the completion of the old International railway, by the late Horace H. French. It is now owned and carried on by his son, C. W. B. French. (*History of Compton County*)

Cookshire House hotel, built by Horace H. French (*History of Compton County*)

Horace married Harriet Bixby Ward on March 5, 1838, in Cookshire. It is understood that they moved to the house now known as 315 Craig St. South in Cookshire in 1838, where generations of the family subsequently lived, and where Eunice French, the mother of John W. French's grandnephew Roger Lancey, was born.

Soon after he was married, Horace was a sergeant in the Sherbrooke Cavalry, as indicated by the pay list reproduced below.

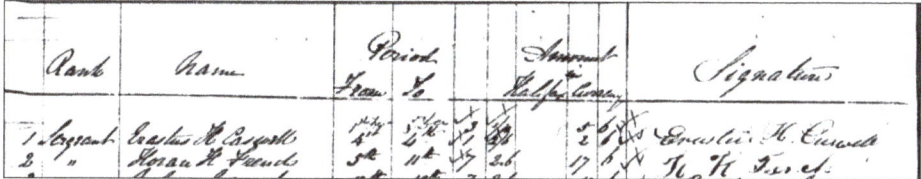

Horace H. French in Sherbrooke Cavalry pay list, December 1838 (ancestry.ca)

Horace Hall French was apparently a very broad-minded and generous man. The *Sherbrooke Record* of October 2, 1940, in an article about a meeting of the Canadian Catholic Historical Association, reported that important donations had been made by non-Catholic friends, including Horace's gift of a piece of land near his house on which to build the church. He and his wife Harriet were strong supporters of St. Peter's Anglican Church in Cookshire – a fact recognized by a memorial stained glass window in the historic church. Horace's gestures of ecumenism also extended to the Methodists:

> The Methodist church, Cookshire, is forty-five by fifty-four feet, and a few years ago was finished throughout in hard wood. The audience room is the largest in the town, seating three hundred persons. The building was erected by Albert Hazeltine, in 1863, at contract price of $2,200. The project of building the church was started in March, 1860, by Rev. T. W. Constable. The first meeting to consider the matter was held in the house of H. H. French. (*History of Compton County*)

Horace and Harriet French memorial window, St. Peter's Church, Cookshire (photos by Linda Hoy)

L. S. Channell noted in his *History of Compton County* that Horace "was one of the chief supporters of the late Honorable John Henry Pope, and always deeply interested in public enterprises." And a November 14, 1890 article in the French language newspaper, *Le Progrès de l'Est*, associated Horace with "The Clique" of Compton County together with Cyrus Bailey, Rufus H. Pope, William Sawyer, Moses Lebourveau and Alexander Ross.

John's father, Charles Ward Bailey French

Charles Ward Bailey French, born at Cookshire in 1845, had a variety of occupations. He was an innkeeper, a farmer, a military man and a politician. He was married twice. His first wife, Maria Bailey, died in 1880, leaving three young children, the youngest of whom was under a month old. His second wife, Catherine McIver, gave birth to seven more children, including John, born in 1888.

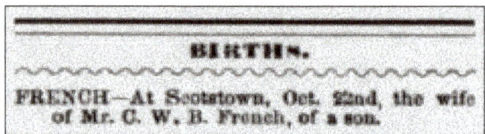

John W. French birth notice (*The Weekly Examiner,* Oct. 26, 1888)

Details of John's siblings and their families are contained in Chapter 9. Charles W.B. French died suddenly on May 18, 1905 at the age of 59 years following a short illness.

Charles W.B. French and family, Scotstown Hotel (*History of Compton County*)

Charles operated the Scotstown Hotel that had been built by his father. In 1899, the hotel experienced a serious fire. A Sherbrooke newspaper reported the conflagration:

> We witnessed the peaceful quietness of the beautiful sunny morning of last Sabbath, 23rd inst., suddenly broken here, when the alarm got up that fire had broken out in the hotel belonging to Mr. Charles French. In a moment all Scotstown was on the scene, bringing out what household furniture could be got out without personal danger, but indeed there were some who ran a great risk in this work. An hour and twenty minutes saw Mr. French, family and boarders with goods turned out without a home.
>
> Much sympathy is felt for Mr. French and large family of young children at this trying time, as their goods have been much damaged in trying to save them, while the house and stables were entirely demolished by the flames . . . Other houses had very narrow escapes. The municipality of Scotstown ought to be looking after a good fire brigade, in case of further casualties. (*Sherbrooke Examiner*, May 1, 1899)

Scotstown Hotel (courtesy of Leslie Buckle)

According to the 1891 Canada Census (for which he was Census Officer for Scotstown), Charles was also a farmer. The *Sherbrooke Examiner* reported that he exhibited swine at the 1893 Compton County Agricultural Society Fair, winning first prize for "Grade sows that have raised pigs."

Charles W. B. French family in 1891 Census, Hampden Township (ancestry.ca)

As did his father Horace, Charles served in the military. In 1873 he was a captain of the Cookshire Cavalry Troop of the Dominion of Canada Militia.

Finally, Charles was a politician. He never succeeded in being elected, though he tried twice. In 1894 he was one of six potential candidates nominated to carry the Conservative banner for Compton County. In the nomination meeting, after 14 ballots, he came up short by a single vote. Three years later, Charles secured the nomination for Compton but was defeated in the general election.

Charles W. B. French, Captain, Dominion of Canada Militia List, 1873 (ancestry.ca)

In spite of Charles's apparent success in life, his wife was left penniless and had to sell off their property when he passed away, as revealed in this legal notice published a few months after his death:

> Be it known that on the fifth day of September, the year one thousand nine hundred and five, in the city of Sherbrooke, St. Francis district, before the undersigned, the Honourable Matthew Hutchinson, Judge of the Superior Court, appeared the petitioner, Dame Catherine McIver, of the city of Scotstown, St. Francis district, widow of the late Charles W. B. French, a farmer and hotelier, of the same place during his lifetime; the said petitioner alleging as follows :
>
> 1. That the said late Charles W. B. French died at the above-mentioned Scotstown, on the thirteenth day of the month of May, the year one thousand nine hundred and five, having made and executed his will in writing before that date, by which he named and constituted the petitioner as his sole and universal legatee, and his executor.
>
> 2. That an inventory of the estate and assets of the said late Charles W. B. French was duly carried out and completed by J. I. Mackie, Notary Public, dated the twenty-sixth day of July 1905.
>
> 3. That, as stated by the said inventory, the estate and businesses of the said late Charles W. B. French are in a sorry state, and that there are not enough assets to cover the liabilities.
>
> 4. That the petitioner did not, in any way, act or accept the said estate.

5. That it is not in the interest of the petitioner to mingle her rights with the obligations of the estate or to accept it, except under the benefit of an inventory. Considering the said petition and the affidavit of the said petitioner, Dame Catherine McIver, we allow and grant to the said Dame Catherine McIver the right, by virtue of the benefit of inventory, to declare and present herself as the heiress of the said late Charles W. B. French and in that capacity, to take possession of all the movable and immovable properties of the said estate, and that she shall be bound only to pay the debts of the said estate to the tune of the amount generated by her property and assets, provided, however, that she has not claimed the inheritance. We give order that the said petitioner Dame Catherine McIver serve a notice of her acceptance to be the universal legatee of the estate of the late Charles W. B. French under the benefit of inventory, by an announcement which must be published twice in *Compton County Chronicle* and *Le Progrès de l'Est*. (*Progrès de l'Est*, Sep. 19, 1905, translated from French by JR Language Translations)

John's mother, Catherine "Kate" McIver

Annie French, Kate McIver, Lottie French
Cookshire, 1916

Left: Kate McIver portrait, ca. 1885; right: Annie French, Kate McIver and Lottie French, 1916 (both courtesy of Ken Watson)

Following are excerpts from Catherine "Kate" MacIver's obituary, published in the *Sherbrooke Daily Record* on December 26, 1933:

Catherine MacIver was born at Red Mountain in 1857 and was married in 1883. Following [husband] Charles' death in 1905, she moved with her two daughters to Humboldt, Minnesota [where her stepfather, Donald

Murray's family had settled] where she resided for four years, then came to Cookshire where she made her home with her son, John.

Her unselfish and kindly manner and generous hospitality endeared her to a large circle of friends . . . [At her funeral at St. Peter's Church, Cookshire] Mr. Tulk spoke words of comfort to the sorrowing family, taking as his theme "The Love of God" to which, he said, a mother's love comes nearest. He also referred to her many acts of kindness to others outside the family circle. . . . (*Sherbrooke Daily Record*, Dec. 26, 1933)

Abandoned Murray farmhouse, Humboldt, Minn., 2019
(photo by Mary Watson)

Kate's family remembers her with much fondness:

Grammy French died before I was born and was much loved by my sisters who knew her. (Alice Wickenden MacEwen)

Catherine is remembered as a gentle person, very sweet-natured. And she was a crackerjack bridge player. (Ken Watson)

My Aunt Alice remembers Grandma French [Kate] speaking Gaelic phrases, and my grandmother Annie (Kate's daughter), speaking a few as well. I was fascinated to learn that – a vestige of the Scottish Hebridean origins of Grandma French, whose mother Isabella (Bella) was born and raised on the Isle of Lewis. According to a book I have (titled *Oatmeal and the Catechism: Scottish Settlers in Quebec* by Margaret Bennett), my great-grandmother Kate would have grown up speaking Gaelic at home, and learned English at school. (Mary Watson)

However, these tributes do not tell the whole story of this remarkably resilient woman. To begin with, she was born of an unknown father – a fact that was very much a family secret until revealed through great-grandnephew Ken Watson's genealogical research in the 1990s. She was raised by her grandparents, Donald MacIver and Mary MacLeod, who were, in some documents, indicated as her parents.

During her life, circumstance caused Kate to be bounced from place to place – from Red Mountain where she was born, to Minnesota in her youth, to Scotstown during her married life, then back to Minnesota following her husband's passing and finally to Cookshire for her twilight years. The second period in Minnesota was especially difficult.

> When Mother and **her** mother and Lottie went to Minnesota after her father died, Mother said that it was very hard for Mama to leave her hard-working sons behind. Horace was in Edmonton, Charlie and Johnny stayed in Compton County. (Alice Wickenden MacEwen)

First name(s)	Last name	Birth year	Birth place	City/township	County	State
Kate	McIver	1858	Canada	Saint Vincent	Kittson	Minnesota

Kate McIver listed in 1880 U.S. Census, Minnesota (ancestry.com)

John Wellington French's middle name

You may have wondered the origin of John's distinguished-sounding middle name. He was named after his uncle, Wellington Horace Orland French, who was born in Cookshire in 1860 and later moved to California. In 1888, he was shot (but not fatally wounded) by Mexican train robbers during a trip south of the border. He died in the USA around 1929.

Wounded by Mexican Bandits.
[*Copyright*, 1888, *by the California Associated Press.*]
AUBURN, June 7th.—W. H. French, who was shot recently in Mexico by train-robbers, was brought to the house of his sister, Mrs. R. F. Rooney. He is improving, though yet quite weak.

Wellington H. French shot in Mexico – *Associated Press,* June 7, 1888 (ancestry.com)

John French's signature is quite unique, in that his middle initial appears to be a lower case "w."

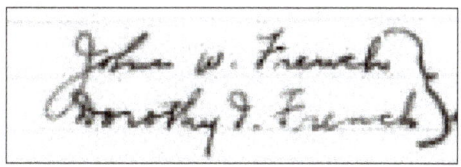

John W. French and Dorothy I. French signatures

Dearly beloved

Chapter 2
The MacLeods: From Lewis to Lingwick

Isle of Lewis (photo by Magz Macleod at Impact Imagz)

The fulmars and guillemots gather
their hosts on the cliffs they enshroud,
to carry my spirit to Lewis;
Innse Gall, dark isle of Macleod.
– © Magz Macleod (Scottish poet/photographer)

(Author's note: To those (like me) whose ornithological knowledge may be limited, or whose Gaelic skills may be found wanting or who may be geographically challenged: despair not. Here are some explanations to fill those gaps without you having to query Google or, heaven forbid, delve into your dusty Merriam-Webster dictionary.

- "fulmars and guillemots" – species of seabirds common to the Scottish Hebrides
- "Innse Gall" – Gaelic name for the Western Isles of Scotland
- "isle of Macleod" – the Isle of Lewis (so referenced because of all the Macleods living there)

The poet's poignant portrayal of the Isle of Lewis personifies the persecution experienced by its people that caused so many to abandon its shores for faraway lands. In this chapter we present a thumbnail history of Clan MacLeod and chronicle the story of Dorothy's ancestors as they overcame onerous obstacles in establishing new lives in Canada's "promised land." In contrast to the French family, which came to Compton County from the United States around 1800, the McLeods came here directly from Scotland about 40 years later.

McLeod/MacLeod/Macleod

There are many different ways to spell this family name, including the three listed. It should be noted that references in this chapter to Dorothy and her ancestors will be spelled differently depending on the various document sources.

Clan history

MacLeod of Lewes dress tartan (ClanMacLeodUSA.org); Clan MacLeod bagpipers (pinterest.com)

Like its distinctive yellow tartan, Clan McLeod has a very colourful history. There are different branches of the clan, including Clan McLeod of Lewis, from which Dorothy is descended. Below is a brief summary of this Scottish highland clan.

> Clan MacLeod of The Lewes, commonly known as Clan MacLeod of Lewis (Scottish Gaelic: Clann Mhic Leòid Leòdhais), is a Highland Scottish clan, which at its height held extensive lands in the Western Isles and west coast of Scotland. From the 14th century up until the beginning of the 17th century there were two branches of Macleods: the MacLeods of Dunvegan and Harris and the Macleods of the Isle of Lewis.
>
> The traditional progenitor of the MacLeods was Leod, made a son of Olaf the Black, King of Mann and the Isles, by a now-discredited tradition. An older, more accepted tradition names his father Olvir and describes the clan as Sliochd Olbhur. Tradition gave Leod two sons, Tormod – progenitor of the Macleods of Harris and Dunvegan (Sìol Thormoid); and Torquil – progenitor of the Macleods of Lewis (Sìol Thorcaill). In the 16th and early 17th centuries, the chiefly line of the Clan Macleod of The Lewes was nearly extinguished by the bloodthirsty and power hungry

chief "Old Rory" and his various offspring. This feuding directly led to the fall of the clan, and loss of its lands to the Clan Mackenzie. One line of the 16th century chiefly family, the Macleods of Raasay, survived and prospered on their lands for centuries thereafter. The current chief of Lewis descends from this latter family.

Today, Clan MacLeod of The Lewes, Clan Macleod of Raasay, and Clan Macleod are represented by "Associated Clan MacLeod Societies," and the chiefs of the three clans. The association is made up of ten national societies around the world including: Australia, Canada, England, France, Germany, New Zealand, Scotland, South Africa, Switzerland, and the United States of America. (wikipedia)

Dorothy – a proud McLeod

Dorothy was a proud McLeod and a "purebred" McLeod because both her parents were McLeods. She and John attended gatherings of the Clan McLeod Association. In 1970, a few months prior to their passing, John and Dorothy sent their regrets at not being able to attend that year's clan gathering.

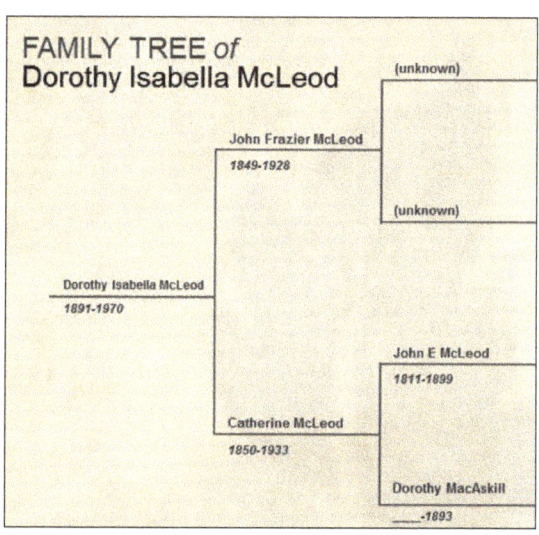

Dorothy I. McLeod family tree pedigree chart (genealogybank.com)

Graniteville, Vermont – Clan MacLeod and Clan MacDonald got together for their annual gathering on Sunday July 19, 1970, at the Alice Macleod farm in Graniteville, Vermont . . . a letter from John W. French in Cookshire was received in which they expressed regret in not being able to attend. (*Sherbrooke Record*, July 30, 1970)

Dorothy's niece, Alice Wickenden MacEwen, vividly recalls an incident in 1961 that demonstrated her Clan McLeod pride:

In August 1961, Mother and Dad, Dorothy and John, my husband Peter and I, my sister Martha and brother-in-law Jim, all went to The Glengarry Highland Games in Maxville, Ont. It was quite an expedition. I remember it as being the year that [Clan Chief] Dame Flora Macleod officially opened the Games. Mother said that Dorothy was in raptures. Every time Dame Flora stood, Aunt Dorothy stood. Macleods Unite! Aunt Dorothy was in a state of absolute bliss. It was a wonderful day for all of us and, I hope, especially for Aunt Dorothy who gave us her patience as sisters-in-law Annie's and Lottie's children took over their summer weeks. (Alice Wickenden MacEwen)

Dorothy's grandfather John E. MacLeod

Dorothy's maternal grandfather, John E. McLeod, was a pioneer in Lingwick Township of Compton County (not far from Eaton Township where her husband John's ancestors had settled). The story of how he ended up there is an interesting one. But first, it is important to paint the

Aunt Dorothy on Cloud Nine at Maxville Highland Games (sketch by James Harvey)

Massed bands, Glengarry Highland Games, Maxville, Ont., 2006 (photo by author)

backdrop to the Scottish immigration of which he was a part:

> In the 1830's, an organization called the British American Land Company (BALC) was sold land in the Eastern Townships by the British government for a pittance on the understanding that the company would use the land for settling English-speakers in those townships before more of the French from the St. Lawrence region moved in.

> The first thirty families that the BALC brought into the Eastern Townships were from England and Ireland in 1835. These settlers were given free passage, money to build homes, furnishings, farming tools, clothes, and food for the first year. They were settled in an area about three miles west of present day Scotstown in an area that was called Victoria. Starting the Victoria settlement and supplying it with enough houses, churches, schools, and government offices stretched the resources available to the BALC. Unfortunately, this first settlement disbanded after just a few years due to the hardships the members encountered and the financial troubles experienced by the BALC because of their generosity.

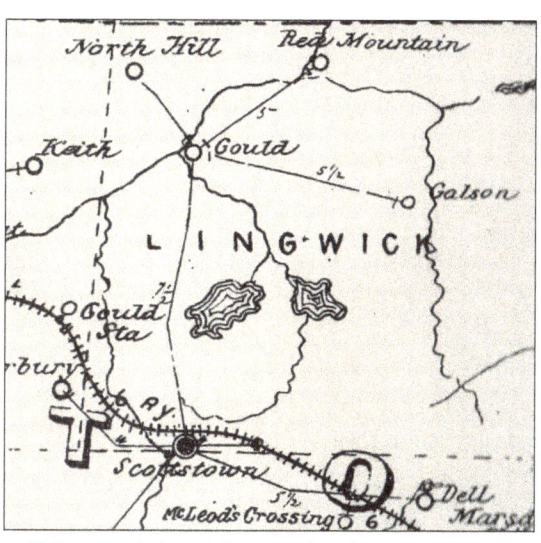

1896 map of Lingwick Township (*History of Compton County*)

> The BALC reduced the amount of its subsidies, but continued to look for people ready to emigrate. There were some parts of Great Britain such as the Scottish Islands and Highlands that were good candidates for immigration due to poverty and hunger caused by factors such as lack of property rights, overcrowding of family farms, and failed crops due to bad weather and disease. (reference: http://hebridscots.com/hisqueb1.htm)

The first Hebridean Scots arrived in 1838 from the Isle of Lewis in the Outer Hebrides of Scotland:

> In 1844 James Matheson, a Scottish Nobleman, bought the Scottish Isle of Lewis for over half a million pounds and built Lews Castle, near Stornoway, clearing more than 500 families off the land by arranging their emigration to Canada. (https://medium.com/@johnkelly_17973/the-highland-clearances-john-d-kelly-phd-b02c9131404c)

Very likely among that initial group was Dorothy's grandfather, John E. McLeod, and probably other members of the McLeod clan. When doing research for this book, I had some difficulty sorting out the different McLeod families of the Lingwick Township region. When I asked long-time area residents Erwin and Muriel Watson if they knew Dorothy's McLeod relatives, they responded "I don't really know . . . there are **so** many McLeods in the area." Indeed! Upon

Isle of Lewis, Scotland
Clockwise from top left: Lewis Castle; sheep farming lands; standing stones, Calanais; shop sign; rocky terrain; restored buildings (photos by author)

subsequent analysis of Lingwick Cemetery records, I discovered that there were a total of 178 McLeods and MacLeods buried there, including 18 whose first name was John! But one gravestone's inscription stood out from all the others:

> **MacLEOD** John E. MacLeod Died 1899, Aged 88 yrs. His Wife Dorothy MacAskill Died 1893 Pioneers from the Isle of Lewis.

It is reassuring to note that I was not alone in finding it difficult to sort out all the MacLeods/McLeods. L.S. Channell, writing in 1896, mentions similar challenges:

Gravestone of John E. MacLeod and Dorothy MacAskill, Lingwick Cemetery (photo by Leslie Nutbrown)

> These [the initial immigrants from Ireland in 1838] were shortly followed by a number of "Highland Scotch" from the island of Lewis. They were Donald MacKay, Murdo MacLean, Donald MacDonald, John MacLeod the horse (so called because he was the only Scotchman who had a horse for the first four years), Malcolm MacLeod, Donald MacLeod, Donald Matheson, Angus MacLeod, and John MacLeod the weaver. There being so many MacLeods and MacDonalds, the Scotch to the present day have many nicknames to distinguish one from the other. (*History of Compton County*)

The newly arrived immigrants faced some formidable challenges as they sought to make new lives for themselves. To many, it must have seemed like a case of jumping from the frying pan into the fire.

> They were probably unaware of the extreme hardships ahead of them. Their deplorable situation in Lewis, however, drove them to emigration – not the lure of Canada as "the Promised Land." . . . Unfortunately, the BALC could not pay for the passage of these Hebridean immigrants. They had to pay for their tickets themselves, but the BALC sold the land to them cheaply and on very favorable terms of interest. They did not have to start paying the Company back until a year after their arrival. In return the settlers agreed to clear one-tenth of the land within four years and to clear a road 20 feet wide in front of their lots. . . . When first settled, this part of the Eastern Townships had no road, was thickly forested with many swampy areas along the Salmon River which flowed through Lingwick. . . . The first few years of the Lewis Scots in Lingwick were indeed difficult ones. (reference: http://hebridscots.com/hisqueb1.htm)

Some of those hardships were described by L.S. Channell in his 1896 book *History of Compton County*:

> The first eight families... all settled on the road between Bury and Gould, as close together as they could. This was always the main thought with the Scotch settlers in those days. ... They wanted to have a settlement of their own, where they could live like Highlanders, 'shoulder to shoulder.' None of them in those days thought of owning a larger farm than fifty acres.
>
> The cabins built by the settlers the first year were very small.... The cabins had no fire places or chimneys the first winter... A hole was made in the roof to let all the smoke out that was inclined to escape. The roof was generally so badly constructed that whenever it rained outside it rained inside also.
>
> The settlers lived the first year principally on oatmeal, advanced by the B.A.L. Company. They paid for this the following summer at the rate of $5 for one hundred pounds, by grubbing out a road from Bury to Gould. (*History of Compton County*)

It wasn't only the emigrants who suffered. Those who were left behind were also negatively impacted, as described by John and Dorothy French's grandniece Mary Watson, who visited the Isle of Lewis in 2018:

> While I had no success tracking down the precise location of the croft that was home to the MacIvers in Lower Barvas, it was both moving and revelatory to walk where my forebears walked, to see the land they were forced to leave in 1851. Most extraordinary, however, was that when a Lewis islander would learn of my connection to the island, almost without exception I'd hear the questions: "How did it turn out for them?" and "Were they alright?" Those questions opened my eyes to the impact of emigration on the islanders left behind – for them, it was a story of loss handed down through the generations, of never knowing the fate of those who left, of communities that were never the same again. In the absence of letters, islanders would have been lucky to have learned anything at all about family and friends forced to emigrate. One person told me that when the ships sailed away from Lewis, islanders stood on the headlands and sang hymns until the ships were out of sight. (Mary Watson)

The "Hercules" emigrant ship from Scottish Hebrides, 1852 (harrisdistillery.com)

Dorothy's father, John F. MacLeod

Dorothy's father, John Frazier McLeod, was born in Gould (Lingwick Township) in 1849 on the farm of his father who, a decade earlier, had emigrated from the Isle of Lewis. As a young man, he served in the 58th Compton Battalion of Infantry during the Fenian Raids. Later, he was a merchant in Lower Town, Bury, for 23 years before retiring to Cookshire in 1921.

John was particularly proud of his military service and was one of four veterans who marched in Bury's Dominion Day parade in 1927 to celebrate Canada's Diamond Jubilee. His personalized Fenian Raids medal is displayed on an Internet medals website. Following is a capsule summary of the Fenian Raids and a detailed description of John's medal:

Gravestone of John F. MacLeod and Catherine MacLeod, Cookshire Cemetery (photo by Leslie Nutbrown)

Fenian raids

The Fenians were a secret society of Irish patriots who had emigrated from Ireland to the United States. Some members of this movement tried to take Canadian territory by force, so they could exchange it with Britain for Irish independence. From 1866 to 1871, the Fenians launched several small, armed attacks. Each raid was put down by government forces. Dozens were killed and wounded on both sides. (https://www.thecanadianencyclopedia.ca/en/article/fenian-raids)

The first infantry company in Compton county was organized March 9, 1866, at Bury. This was brought about through the instrumentality of Captain F. M. Pope, who was at the time attending the military school in Montreal. Those in authority were aware of the intended Fenian raids and commenced to prepare accordingly. Captain Pope, who was then only a young man, by request left the school and started at once for his home, where, in a few months, he organized no less than four companies of infantry. (*History of Compton County*)

John's Fenian Raids medal is officially described as follows by a website that specializes in all types of historical military medals:

Circular silver medal on swivel ribbon bar with original 'FENIAN RAID 1870' clasp; the face with the veiled head and shoulders portrait of Queen Victoria facing left, circumscribed 'VICTORIA REGINA ET IMPERATRIX' (Victoria Queen and Empress), signed 'T.B.' (for the sculptor Sir Thomas Brock KCB, RA, 1847-1922 whose most famous works include the statue of Prince Albert for the Albert Memorial at Kensington and the Imperial Memorial to Queen Victoria in front of Buckingham Palace); the reverse with the then Canadian flag within a wreath of maple leaves, inscribed 'CANADA' above; attributed on the edge to 'Pte. J. F. McLeod 58th Bn.', the initials officially corrected; on replaced correct ribbon.

The Medal was instituted by the Canadian government as late as January 1899 to be awarded to the Canadian and British forces that had confronted the Fenian and Red River raids of 1866 and 1870 by dissident Irish Americans from across the border. Volunteers from the 53rd Sherbrooke Battalion, the 54th Richmond Battalion and the 58th Compton Battalion formed a company that served in the Fenian Raids of 1870. (http://www.medal-medaille.com)

John F. McLeod Fenian Raid medal; personalized name clasp (medal-medaille.com)

John McLeod was a strong supporter of First World War relief efforts. In January 1915 he was appointed to the Belgian Relief Committee. On April 17, 1915, the *Sherbrooke Daily Record* reported that he had made a very generous donation of $50 (equivalent to $1200 in today's terms) to the Red Cross.

> The Sherbrooke Branch of the Canadian Red Cross Society gratefully acknowledges from Mr. J. F. McLeod of Bury, the sum of $50 to install a bed in the Duchess of Connaught's Canadian Red Cross Hospital at Cliveden [England] under the name of J. F. McLeod and his two daughters, Eva M. McLeod and Dorothy I. McLeod. (*Sherbrooke Daily Record*, Apr. 17, 1915)

Like John French's father, Dorothy's father was also involved in politics. In the lead-up to the 1917 federal election, he was appointed the official agent for candidate Aylmer Byron Hunt, who subsequently won the Compton County seat. However, there was one big difference – John's father was a Conservative, while Dorothy's dad was a Liberal!

Now that we have covered their respective ancestors, we will turn our focus to John and Dorothy themselves.

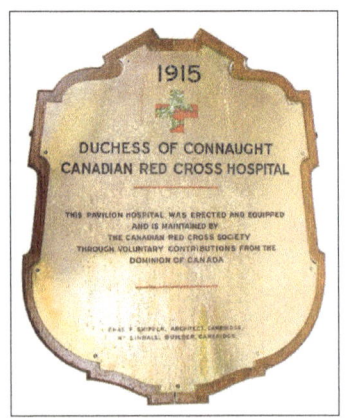

Duchess of Connaught Canadian Red Cross Hospital plaque (redcross.ca)

Chapter 3
John: A Man of Many Hats

Home is where you hang your hat. — Leon Redbone (American singer/songwriter)

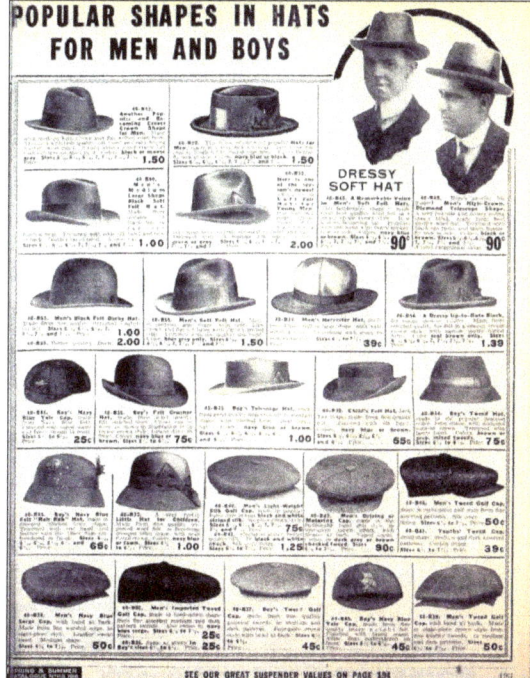 

Vintage ad for men's hats (pinterest.com); John French dressed up for Old Home Week, Cookshire (courtesy of Leslie Buckle)

John French had many hats to hang – hats that he accumulated during his 47 years of unmarried life. This is not too surprising, given that both his father and his grandfather were also multi-taskers as they divided their time among farming, entrepreneurial and community involvement activities.

Before I began doing research for this book, I had little idea of what John did during his working life – apart from his two-year stint as a Member of Quebec's Legislative Assembly. And I was not alone in my ignorance. Neither my siblings nor John's nieces and nephews knew exactly what his work had been. Even some of **his** own siblings weren't sure. Niece Alice recalls such an instance:

When Mother ([John's sister] Annie Eliza Catherine French Wickenden) seemed at a loss to tell me what Uncle John "did," I decided that it was somehow mixed up with French's Mustard. She did not like condiments such as ketchup and mustard. Our relishes were homemade and highly prized! There was a small jar of mustard in a kitchen cupboard that was seldom used. Mother said that meat should stand on its own, sans condiments save horseradish for Dad. Once in a while, a roast of beef would be topped with a crust of homemade mustard paste. Occasionally mustard appeared in a little glass dish at the table. Later, as a daughter or two "did the dishes," she would spoon out the remaining mustard from its table dish and as she whacked the spoon against the jar whence it came, she would say "That's how the mustard company makes its money." "How can she say that?" I would wonder – especially when it's a family business! (Alice Wickenden MacEwen)

French's mustard jar (collectorsjournal.com)

But, alas, I discovered that John actually **did** work. So now let's take a look at some of the hats, caps and other headwear that he was known to have worn in the years prior to his marriage to Dorothy.

Farmer

Farmer's cap (ebay.com)

Farming apparently was one of John's first occupations. In a 1954 interview with the *Sherbrooke Record*, it was reported "The years 1910, 1911 and 1912 were spent out West, where he farmed." No additional details were provided. Therefore, the exact nature of John's farming activities remains a mystery in spite of extensive efforts to find out more. Although admittedly they result from pure speculation, there are at least three possible scenarios.

Given that his older brother, Horace, moved out west to Wetaskiwin, Alta., in November 1909 to work in C. C. Bailey's jewellery store, it is possible that John followed a few months later and went into farming in that same general area.

A second hypothesis is related to the fact that John's widowed mother and his two younger sisters moved to Minnesota in 1905, where they lived with the former's stepfather's family. Perhaps John joined them some years later, or he might have used the area as a launching point for settling on a farm across the border in Manitoba.

A third possibility is that John went West on a "harvest excursion" and ended up staying there for a couple of years. These excursion trips were very popular among the young men of Cookshire and elsewhere in the Eastern Townships. John's future father-in-law, John F. McLeod, was one of those who joined the excursion around that time. My own dad answered the call of the west some years later. And many years after that, John's nephew, Donald French, had a very abbreviated Harvest Excursion experience:

> I went out West on the harvest excursion one year, but it lasted only 10 days. On my second week there, it snowed a foot, causing an immediate halt to the harvest. So we were all sent back home. That was the end of it! (Don French)

HARVESTERS EXCURSIONS.

The Canadian Pacific Railway will shortly inaugurate their annual Harvesters' Excursion to Western Canada and it is expected that, as in previous years, thousands will avail themselves thereof to visit Manitoba, Saskatchewan and Alberta. The programme of the special trains has not yet been finally completed, but it seems settled that seperate excursions will run from the Maritime Provinces and the Provinces of Quebec and Ontario, full particulars of which will be announced in the course of a few days. Meantime, prospective excursionists who might be in need of information are invited to correspond with the nearest Canadian Pacific Railway agent, when full particulars will be sent as soon as the dates of the excursion have been finally decided upon.

Harvester Excursion ad (*Quebec Chronicle*, Aug. 8, 1910)

As a farming postscript, we do know that John raised chickens while living in Cookshire and exhibited them at the 1921 Cookshire Fair, winning second prize.

> PRIZE LIST OF COOKSHIRE FAIR: POULTRY: (Orpington – Black Minorca – Dorking): Pullet—1st N. Roux, 2nd J. W. French, 3rd O.F. Bailey. (*Sherbrooke Daily Record*, Oct. 10, 1921)

Whatever the type of full-time farming that John engaged in and wherever it happened, it still seems an unlikely occupation for someone who appeared to be

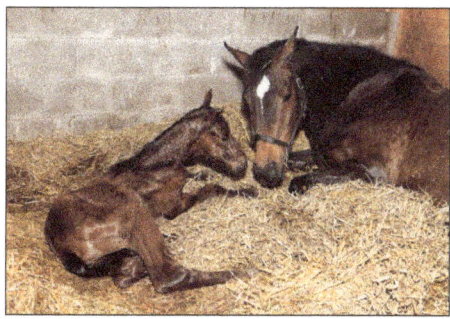

Left: newborn colt (istockphoto; credit purple_queue)
Right: Sow and newborn piglets (istockphoto; credit umsama)

more comfortable in a suit, tie and brogues than in overalls and rubber boots. Nevertheless, I discovered that in later years, John was occasionally involved in farming activities on my dad's farm in Cookshire, as revealed by my mom's and grandmother's diary entries. Obviously, John must have acquired his animal husbandry skills somewhere!

- June 2, 1939: John French helped with birth of colt (Lilla J. Fraser's diary)
- Mar. 21, 1950: Pigs starting arriving at 8:30 AM. 12 in all (one died). John French stayed until midnight so Dad could sleep (Alice Fraser's diary)

Vintage hardhat (troutunderground.com)

Contractor

Beginning in the late 1910s, through the 1920s and into the 1930s, John worked as a general contractor, specializing in the construction of roads, bridges and railroads. Although he executed some of the projects on his own, others were realized in collaboration with his older brother, Charles, who was president of Kennedy Construction Company of Montreal. John's nephew, Don French, who later took over Kennedy Construction, explained to me that they would sometimes "farm out" projects to John. Many years later, John worked as a foreman on one of his nephew-in-law John Wickenden's construction projects in Three Rivers (Trois-Rivières).

One of John's first solo projects involved major road construction in the Beauce region of Quebec. Several references to this work appeared in local newspapers:

COOKSHIRE: Mr. John French is in town from St. Romaine [Beauce], the guest of his mother, Mrs. C. W. B. French (*Sherbrooke Daily Record*, July 2, 1919)

ST-ROMAINE: Our road work, under the supervision of our contractor, Mr. J. W. French, is moving ahead quickly; let's hope that before long, we will be able to make the trip from Beauce to Sherbrooke more rapidly. (*La Tribune*, Sep. 11, 1919, translated by author)

ST-ROMAIN DE WINSLOW: Mr. J. W. French, road contractor, has come to look over the work in preparation for the hauling of gravel. (*La Tribune*, Dec. 2, 1919, translated by author)

ST-ROMAINE: Our road work on the Beauceville to Sherbrooke Highway is now completed. Our contractor, Mr. J. W. French, has only a few days work left for his employees to repair a bridge. (*La Tribune*, May 28, 1921, translated by author)

John's road construction company was mentioned in the debates of the Quebec Legislative Assembly in 1922:

> For the province's highway network, the following entrepreneurs have signed contracts with the government in 1921 and 1922: . . . J. W. French (www.assnat.qc.ca)

A more local project carried out by John's company involved the replacement of the Munn Bridge over the Eaton River near Sawyerville.

1941 Postcard of Munn's Bridge, built by John French in 1926 (author's collection)

> TENDERS WANTED: Tenders will be received, up to 12 o'clock noon, by the Municipal Council of Newport, at a meeting held on March 1st, 1926, for the building of a steel bridge (to replace the old one) across the South Branch of the Eaton River, known as the Munn Bridge, about one mile from the Village of Sawyerville in accordance with plans, specifications and regulations furnished by the Department of Public Works and Labor.
>
> Tenders will be received for the superstructure and substructure together or separately. No contract will be entered into for the building of this bridge until the passing of a by-law by the Council ordering the work to be done, and of its approval by the ratepayers of the Municipality. Plans and specifications may be seen at the office of the Sec.-Treas. Lowest or any tender not necessarily accepted. (*Sherbrooke Daily Record*, Feb. 15, 1926)
>
> ISLAND BROOK: At a recent meeting of the Council to receive the tenders for building the Munn bridge, the tender of Mr. John W. French of Cookshire, was accepted for the sum of nine thousand and six hundred and sixty-four dollars. (*Sherbrooke Daily Record*, Mar. 11, 1926)

In another bridge project, even closer to home, John worked with his brother Charles to replace the Main Street bridge in Cookshire.

> COOKSHIRE BRIDGE CONSTRUCTION: The French company, of Cookshire, has begun construction of a bridge over the Eaton River, near the Ashby garage. This company was awarded the contract last year to replace the old bridge that was built of wood and iron and crossed the river at the same location. Since the beginning of the project, workers have been busy building temporary pillars to support the old bridge during the construction of the new one. Until now, vehicles have been forced to make a detour of two miles and a half via Slab City or of ten miles by [East] Angus. (*La Tribune*, June 18, 1936, translated by author)

Bridge over Eaton River at Cookshire, 2020 (photo by author)

Among other major projects undertaken by John French were ones in Vaudreuil in 1923 and Blind River, Ont., in 1929. In spite of The Great Depression, it appears that his contracting business was still able to continue during those difficult economic times.

Businessman

As a contractor, John was obviously a businessman as well. In fact, a newspaper reference to his Blind River project appears to suggest that he was there for other reasons as well:

Businessman's hat

Mr. John W. French is in Blind River, where he expects to remain for a few weeks looking after his business interests. (*Sherbrooke Daily Record*, May 11, 1929)

Be that as it may, there are other reasons to consider him a businessman. In the 1920 Deed of Purchase for his Main Street home, John's occupation was specified as "automobile dealer."

John French was also very involved in the business of the Town of Cookshire, serving as a councillor from 1925 to 1935. He had been unanimously elected to replace the late Mr. Ayton Cromwell. One of John's contributions on the Council was his proposal of a motion to request that the Quebec Liquor Commission grant two tavern permits.

Philanthropist

Definition: philanthropist: one who desires to promote the welfare of others, expressed especially by the generous donation of money to good causes.

Not to be compared with the great philanthropists of our time, such as Bill Gates and Warren Buffett, John French was

J. W. French's Cookshire Town Council motion re tavern licences (*Sherbrooke Daily Record*, Feb. 28, 1927)

nonetheless a bona fide philanthropist. Often, it is later in life that a person's philanthropic actions become prominent. However, in John French's case, they began early and would increase significantly during his retirement years, as will be detailed in Chapter 8. Following are several examples of his early support of various types of community causes.

In 1921, John was a major sponsor of the efforts to start a Compton County Fair, donating $40 ($500 in today's terms).

In 1926, John made a significant donation to the Scotstown Memorial Library's subscription campaign:

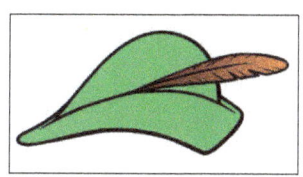

Robin Hood hat

Additional subscribers to the "Scotstown Memorial Library" are the following: Mrs. Norreys Hunting, Morin Heights $2; Mrs. Kenneth Nicholson, North Hill $2.; Miss Evelyn Bennett, $2; Rev. E. M. W. Templeman, $1; Mr. John W. French, Cookshire, $5. (*Sherbrooke Daily Record*, Apr. 29, 1926)

When the Cookshire Cemetery Association was reorganized in 1928, John's support of fundraising efforts for the cemetery's upkeep was recognized by him being named to the Board of Trustees. Further details of his support of the cemetery are contained in Chapter 13.

Youth leader

John was always fond of young people and concerned about their welfare. It is not surprising, then, that as a young man he became involved in youth leadership activities. A brief news item in the *Sherbrooke Daily Record* tells how it began.

> A special illustrated lecture on the Boy Scout movement was delivered in the [St. Peter's Church] Parish Hall on Tuesday evening by Mr. E. Russell Patterson, General Provincial Secretary of the Province of Quebec. Two patrols were organized with Cyrus and John French as patrol leaders. (*Sherbrooke Daily Record*, Mar. 27, 1914)

Compton County Agricultural Society appeal (*Sherbrooke Daily Record*, Mar. 16, 1921)

Scout hat (worthpoint.com)

It is important to understand that the Scouting movement had only begun a few years earlier in the UK and had just been incorporated in Canada.

The scouting movement was founded in England in 1907 by Robert Baden-Powell, then a lieutenant-general in the British army. Scouting came to Canada in early 1908 with three troops established almost simultaneously in Merrickville and St Catharines, Ont. and Port Morien, N.S, and in 1912 the Boy Scout Association was granted a royal charter throughout the Commonwealth by King George V. (thecanadianencyclopedia.ca)

The purpose of the Scout Movement is to contribute to the development of young people in achieving their full physical, intellectual, emotional, social and spiritual potentials as individuals, as responsible citizens and as members of their local, national and international communities. (wikipedia.com)

One of the first activities of the newly formed Cookshire Scout patrols was a 10-day campout at Silver Lake.

In addition to his leadership role with the Boy Scouts, John accompanied youth in other community activities. Below is a report of one such instance:

> COOKSHIRE: Several of the High School boys accompanied by Mr. S. N. Pergau and Mr. J. W. French, motored to Scotstown on June 1st to attend the sports day exercises. (*Sherbrooke Daily Record*, June 8, 1929)

COOKSHIRE BOY SCOUTS IN CAMP

TENTS ARE PITCHED ON ISLAND AT SILVER LAKE — PRACTICAL WORK CARRIED ON

Marbleton, July 16—(Special)—Two patrols of Boy Scouts from Cookshire have been camping at Silver Lake for the last ten days. The boys pitched their tents on the Island, and have the Silver Lake Club House at their disposal, besides three boats, one of which is the property of the Scouts. A special training course in Scout Craft has been carried on by Mr. A.C. Carter, expert director from Quebec, and lately from England. Mr. Carter was one of the first Scouts to join the movement. Besides Mr. Carter, a special staff, consisting of Mr. Douglas Sellars, of Richmond, Mr. Thomas Burton, of Cookshire; Mr. Ayton Cromwell, President of the Cookshire local Association of Scouts; and the Rev. E.R. Roy, Scoutmaster of the Cookshire troops, have been in camp helping the boys.

Cyrus and John French are the two Patrol leaders; Alex. and Douglas Taylor, the two Corporals; Ross Cromwell, Secretary; and Wyatt Johnston, Special troop bugler. A large number of parents, and others interest in the movement have visited the boys in camp.

John French is patrol leader at Silver Lake Boy Scout camp (*Sherbrooke Daily Record*, July 18, 1914)

Sportsman

Although one would not necessarily think of John as a sportsman or an athlete, the historical record/*Record* indicates otherwise:

> MASSAWIPPI: The Messrs. Thomas Burton, Cyrus and John French, John Burton, Wyatt Johnson, Alex Taylor and Ross Cromwell, campers at "Castlewood," Perkin's Point, Lake Massawippi, the past two weeks, left on Tuesday, after a fine holiday time, for their respective homes at Cookshire. (*Sherbrooke Daily Record*, July 29, 1919)

> Messrs. John French and John Burton have returned from a fortnight's camping at Lake Massawippi (*Sherbrooke Daily Record*, Aug. 11, 1921)

> Mr. Emmett Leonard, of Toronto, Ont., Mr. John W. French, Mr. W. H. Leonard and Mr. Charles Baker spent Thursday and Friday, July 7 and 8, fishing at Lac Tortue. (*Sherbrooke Daily Record*, July 15, 1932)

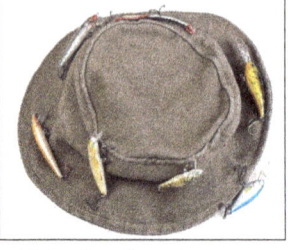

Fishing hat (istockphoto, credit shiffti); hockey toque (fanatics.com)

John French and John Burton went fishing in PM. Caught 9. (Alice Fraser's diary, June 12, 1949)

It is possible that John also played hockey. The report of a local match between Cookshire and Birchton lists the Cookshire goalkeeper simply as "French." Also, in a circa 1920 photograph of the Cookshire hockey team, one of John's nieces identified the goalkeeper as **possibly** being her Uncle John.

COOKSHIRE DEFEATED BIRCHTON

COOKSHIRE, March 13.—With a very good attendance and an excellent representation from Birchton, Cookshire defeated the Birchton team on Friday evening playing at the Cookshire Hockey Club Rink by a score of 6 to 4. The game was handled by Mr John E. Drennan, Jr., and the teams lined-up as follows:

Cookshire (6)		Birchton (4)
French	Goal	Picard
S. Woolley	Defence	H. Picard
Morgan	Defence	Taylor
Migneault	Centre	Rogers
Johnston	R. Wing	G. Picard
Gadley	L. Wing	Sevigny
F. Woolley	Subs.	Giroux
Seale	"	

"French" hockey goalkeeper, Cookshire (*Sherbrooke Daily Record*, Mar. 13, 1923)

Cookshire town hockey team, ca. 1920 (Fraser family archives)

Caregiver

No, John French was not a nurse! In fact, he could **not** have been a nurse at that time because men were barred from entering that noblest of professions. However, he was definitely a caregiver, as demonstrated by a sampling of the

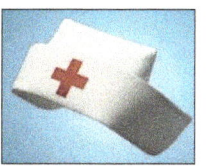
Nursing cap (pinterest.com)

caring deeds that characterized his life.

First of all, John was a caregiver to his family. Only 17 years old at the time of his father's passing, he suddenly inherited the caregiving role – especially with respect to his mother and his little sister Annie. In later years, he became responsible for the care of his two half-sisters, Pertie and Ellen.

In June 1931, John declined the Conservative nomination for Compton County, most likely because he needed to care for his ailing mother.

John's caring outreach extended beyond family into the community. One example of his caring gestures was that he frequently served as a casket bearer when someone in the community passed away. Caregiving – in all its forms – was certainly a part of John's DNA. In the words of his niece, Martha, "Uncle John was thoughtful of others – always."

Later in life, John would become a recipient of care, as he confronted a number of medical issues, some of which were alluded to or mentioned in newspaper social notes or my mom's diary entries:

> Mr. and Mrs. John W. French have returned to their home, after spending the winter months in Montreal. Mr. French's friends will be pleased to know he has improved in health (*Sherbrooke Daily Record*, Apr. 12, 1938)

> Mr. and Mrs. John W. French spent a few weeks in Bronxville, New York, as guests of Mrs. French's sister, Mrs. H. W. Shirreffs, and Mr. Shirreffs. Mr. French was also in Boston [for treatment]. (*Sherbrooke Daily Record*, Oct. 24, 1940)

Extract from Annie French Wickenden letter to daughter Alice, ca. 1960 (courtesy of Alice Wickenden MacEwen)

> Mr. John French has returned from the Royal Victoria Hospital, Montreal, where he spent several weeks as a patient. (*Sherbrooke Daily Record*, Sep. 22, 1942)

> John French had rupture operation yesterday AM (Alice Fraser's diary, Mar. 19, 1963)

Chauffeur

To say that John was a chauffeur might hinge a bit too heavily on hyperbole, but he did have a strong affinity with the motorcar. The anecdotal evidence that follows will serve to demonstrate that the chauffeur's cap does indeed fit.

The *Sherbrooke Daily Record* reported on May 13, 1914, that John French had purchased a new car. It didn't say what kind of car he bought, but we were to learn later the model – a brand spanking new McLaughlin car. In case you, like me, have never heard of a McLaughlin car, here is a brief history of the vehicle:

1914 McLaughlin 1 (antique.vccc.com)

McLaughlin Motor Car Company Limited was a Canadian manufacturer of automobiles headquartered in Oshawa, Ontario. The company was founded by Robert McLaughlin as a [horse] carriage manufacturing company. By 1915 McLaughlin produced one carriage every ten minutes. In 1907 the business grew to include the manufacture of McLaughlin automobiles with Buick engines and in 1915, with the addition of Chevrolet vehicles, the carriage end of the business was sold to the Carriage Factories Ltd. of Orillia, Ontario. McLaughlin was acquired by General Motors in 1918. (wikipedia.com)

Sadly, a few years later, John's fancy horseless carriage was stolen from his driveway. But grieve not, that story has a happy ending:

Alfred Roy and Walter Trepanier, of Magog, have been arrested by the Cookshire police, charged with the theft of the McLaughlin touring car, the property of Mr. J. W. French, of Cookshire, which was stolen in Cookshire on Thursday. (*Sherbrooke Daily Record*, Oct. 10, 1925)

MOTOR STOLEN AT COOKSHIRE IS RECOVERED

Two Magog Men Held by Police as Being Responsible for Theft —Will Appear Before Judge Lemay.

Alfred Roy and Walter Trepanier, of Magog, have been arrested by the Cookshire police, charged with the theft of the McLaughlin touring car, the property of Mr. J. W. French, of Cookshire, which was stolen in Cookshire on Thursday. They were brought to Sherbrooke last evening, and are being held here, awaiting their appearance before Judge J. H. Lemay in the Magistrate's Court.

John W. French car stolen and recovered (*Sherbrooke Daily Record*, Oct. 10, 1925)

Chauffeur cap (etsy.com)

John's car got a lot of use as he chauffeured family and friends, "motoring" here, there and everywhere – both locally and afar – as reported in the *Record's* trusty social notes columns:

John French motored here [Foster] on Sunday from Cookshire. (*Sherbrooke Daily Record*, June 23, 1923)

> Mr. John French has returned from a six weeks' trip to the Pacific coast. He was accompanied by his brother, Mr. Charles D. French, of Westmount. They spent some time with their brother, Mr. Horace A. French, at Wetaskiwin, Alta. (*Sherbrooke Daily Record*, Mar. 10, 1924)
>
> Mr. John W. French, Mrs. Charles W. B. French, Mrs. John W. Robinson and Miss Ellen French motored to Scotstown on Monday last to attend the funeral of the late Mrs. W. A. Ladd. (*Sherbrooke Daily Record*, Sep. 10, 1924)
>
> John French motored to Three Rivers and spent the week-end with Mr. and Mrs. J. Wickenden and family. (*Sherbrooke Daily Record*, Aug. 21, 1929)
>
> Mr. Malcolm Mackenzie and four daughters, the Misses Mary, Margaret, Ruth and Rhona, who have spent three weeks at the home of the former's mother, Mrs. C. W. B. French, returned to their home in Montreal West, on Friday last. Mr. J. W. French motored to Montreal with them, returning home on Saturday. (*Sherbrooke Daily Record*, Sep. 12, 1929)

But the crowning glory of John's career as a chauffeur happened in July of 1928, when he had the singular honour of chauffeuring Opposition Leader (and soon to be Prime Minister) R. B. Bennett on his campaign visit to Cookshire. The *Record* reported details of the event:

> The Hon. R. B. Bennett, leader of the Opposition, completed his tour of the Eastern Townships on Sunday morning after paying a visit of six days to this part of the Province of Quebec, the most extensive tour ever made in the district by a leader of a political party in Canada. Mr. Bennett ended his travels, as far as this territory was concerned, at Cookshire. . . During the day, they motored from one end of Compton County to the other, addressing five meetings . . . Mr. Bennett and Miss Bennett were accompanied throughout the day by a squadron of eight or ten motors, and while Mr. Bennett travelled with Mr. John French of Cookshire, Miss Bennett was with Senator and Mrs. Pope. (*Sherbrooke Daily Record*, July 3, 1928)

Politician

John French's successful foray into the political arena in the 1950s is well known. The details of that adventure will be covered in Chapter 7. However, you may not know about John's earlier political involvement. In July 1928, as indicated above, he actively supported the

Politician's hat (gentlemansgazette.com, adapted by author)

campaign of Conservative leader R. B. Bennett and was very visible during Bennett's visit to Compton County.

In June 1931 he was a leading candidate for the Conservative nomination for Compton County:

> Active preparations are being made by the Conservative forces in Compton County for the forthcoming provincial elections. . . [It was decided to] hold a convention here [in Cookshire] next Monday when the candidate will be chosen. Although the executive have not placed approval on any individual, several names are prominently mentioned in connection with the candidacy. John French of Cookshire, is the most popularly mentioned. Family reasons, however, are understood to stand in his way and the selection possibly lies between W. H. Hill of Bulwer, and P. A. Sherman, of Scotstown. (*Sherbrooke Daily Record*, June 26, 1931)

Ultimately, the nomination went to P. A. Sherman. It is believed that the "family reasons" cited above were related to the health of John's mother, with whom he was living. She passed away in 1933.

John remained involved in politics at the federal level. In 1934, he was appointed Compton County revising officer to prepare voters' lists.

Performer

Performer's hat (wikipedia.com)

Although this hat spent most of its time on the hat rack, we discovered two occasions when John put it on. These instances were obviously preludes to his later post-marital "performances" when he would build his reputation as a great entertainer.

The first occasion goes back to when John was just 12 years old and attending Scotstown Academy. A local paper describes the event:

> COMPTON COUNTY FALL SHOW, SCOTSTOWN: The Fall show of the Compton County Agricultural Association No. 2 was held on Friday Sept. 13th and was a decided success. . . Special interest was taken in the testing of the horses pulling the heavy stone drag. . . In the evening, a "Templar" Silver medal contest was held in the Town Hall. The following are the names of the contestants and their recitations: . . . "The Farmer and his Gun," Master John French . . . The recitations were well rendered and in almost every case showed good elocutionary power. (*Sherbrooke Examiner*, Sep. 18, 1901)

Author's note: An Internet search turned up the following words as the first verse of John's recitation:

A smart young fox sat airing his view in dingly dell one night,
I'm glad to see that human folk at last set things a right,
Abolish all blood sports they say, and down with hunting men!!
What rubbish are you quoting?
Said an old grey fox just then.
Young man I'm old and grey I know,
My coat is stained and worn,
But the song I always love to hear is the tune of a hunting horn.
Your foolish talk may sound quite fine, to ignorant folk or dull,
But to foxes who have lived some years their fears it will not lull.
Yes fears my friend for look you here if our hunting friends do go,
There'll be the farmer and his gun, he'll be a bitter foe.

John's next documented performance occurred many years later in 1929, again in Scotstown:

The Gaelic concert held in the Odd Fellows' Hall on Friday evening, June 7th, proved most successful. . . Messrs. Kenneth MacLeod and J. French, of Cookshire, sang some English songs, Harry Lauder's proving favourites with the audience. They also sang duets, receiving insistent encores. A number of Scotch song choruses were given. . . The proceeds from the concert amounted to nearly seventy dollars. Dancing was indulged in for a few hours. (*Sherbrooke Daily Record*, June 17, 1929)

Author's note: Among the popular Harry Lauder songs that John might have performed: "Roamin' in the Gloamin," "A Wee Deoch-an-Doris," "The End of the Road" and "I Love a Lassie."

Around the same time, it appears that John was quite involved with the Social Club of the local Anglican church, as indicated in the following report. However, it is not known whether he actually "performed" at any of their events.

COOKSHIRE: At the [St. Peter's] Parish Hall on Wednesday evening, February 6th, the first address was delivered of the series arranged for by the social club of St. Peter's Church. The Rector, the Rev. A. W. Buckland, introduced the speaker, Dr. A. Johnston, who gave a highly interesting and scholarly address on the topic of "Science and Religion." . . . At the close of this splendid address, Mr. F. E. Kerridge moved a vote of thanks to Dr. Johnston. . . This motion was seconded by Mr. John W. French. (*Sherbrooke Daily Record*, Feb. 9, 1929)

The missing headgear

Among John's copious collection of cranium crowns, there was one missing – the army helmet. Given the impressive record of military service of his ancestors, his family and his Cookshire contemporaries, one might have expected John to follow in their footsteps. After all, he was the right age, being only 26 years old when World War I broke out. So why did he not "go to war"? As I learned from his family, it definitely was not from a lack of patriotism. His nephew, John Wickenden, assumed that it was due to a medical condition. Niece Alice Wickenden MacEwen provided additional details:

Canadian army helmet, World War I (thestar.com)

> I spoke to John, brother, yesterday and we surmised that Uncle John did not "go to war" (as we used to say) because of his eyesight, his very crossed eye or eyes. As a child, to me, Uncle John's eyes were HIS EYES. As were Aunt Lottie's. Strabismus was a word not known to us, nor was the problem ever mentioned. As time went by, I noticed that some of us Wickendens had the same problem – Jean and John, pronounced; Martha and Alice, only now and then. Both Jean and John had surgery, Jean twice. My son Will has a flicker of strabismus and his daughter Mary too. I know that Mother's father had a very crossed eye. (Alice Wickenden MacEwen)

Bye, bye hats!

Although many of John French's hats described above would be destined to gather dust for the rest of his life, a few special ones would come in handy during his retirement years. You will discover which ones in Chapter 8.

Chapter 4
Dorothy: A Woman With Class

Without teachers, life would have no class. – JH Notebooks

One-room schoolhouse (istockphoto; credit pabradyphoto)

The double entendre of this chapter's title is intentional and, in this case, both meanings are positive. Firstly, Dorothy was known to friends and family as a classy woman. She was a very smart dresser and always conducted herself with the utmost of grace. Her constant smile illumined her surroundings, and her calm personality engendered reassurance that all was well.

Secondly, she spent much of her early life in class – first as a student, then as a teacher – where she was party to a plethora of pedagogical programs, practices and proceedings, some of which were quite unique. This chapter traces Dorothy's life and career up until her marriage to John in 1935.

Early years

Because of the almost complete absence of extant documentation, we know practically nothing about Dorothy's childhood. All we do know, from her obituary, is that she was born in Gould (Lingwick Township) on May 11, 1891, and that her family moved to Bury "when she was quite young." We also learn that she attended Bury Model School and Bury Academy.

Everything else is left to one's imagination. That being the case, I invited members of her family to imagine what little Dorothy (or Belle, as she was sometimes called) might have been like as a young girl:

> I imagine Aunt Dorothy would have been a gentle, well-behaved little girl, always kind and obedient and NOT mischievous. (Martha Wickenden MacKellar)

> I would think she would have been kind and intelligent; a caring sort of person and a good friend. (John French Wickenden)

> I think Aunt Dorothy was a quiet girl, well aware of her intelligence, who chose to join the "work force" as evidenced by her careers. Her last career was Uncle John, her other heart's desires having been fulfilled. (Alice Wickenden MacEwen)

Based on how I personally remember my godmother as an adult, I will offer my own impression of what she might have been like as a child. The first adjectives that come to mind are perky, pretty and precocious. Perhaps she also possessed some of the personality traits of another young girl named Dorothy – of The Wizard of Oz fame: cute, curious and compassionate.

Dorothy's obituary contains a single sentence that reveals something she did, likely during her teenage years.

> While living in Bury, she attended the old Methodist Church and taught in the Sunday School. (Dorothy French obituary, *Sherbrooke Daily Record*, June 26, 1970)

As a postscript to this section, I will share one little tidbit of information that I did find from Dorothy's early childhood. In 1899, when Dorothy would have been eight years old, the *Sherbrooke Examiner* reported on a gathering in Keith (near Bury).

> The lamp which was in the possession of the "Ladies Aid" of Keith was disposed of [raffled off] at the home of Mr. M. F. McLeod on Monday evening where a few were gathered, which fell to the lot of Mrs. Norman McLeod, of same place, also a whip which fell to the lot of Miss Belle McLeod, of Bury. (*Sherbrooke Examiner*, Sep. 20, 1899)

Methodist Church, Robinson (Bury), ca. 1900 (McCord Museum, courtesy of Joel Barter)

Dorothy: A Woman With Class

Sunday School teacher (kidology.org)

What Dorothy would have done with such an unusual prize is not obvious. At her tender age, she probably did not yet drive a horse and buggy, in which case the whip could have been useful to tickle the tail of a lazy equine. Perhaps it could have come in handy for schoolroom discipline a few years later when she would have embarked on her teaching career. Or heaven forbid that the need should ever occur to keep an eventual cantankerous husband in check! However, given Dorothy's personality, the whip most likely was kept as an unused souvenir of a bygone era.

Macdonald College

Dorothy's next appearance in print occurred in 1911 when we discover that she was enrolled in the teacher training course at Macdonald College in Ste. Anne de Bellevue at the western end of the island of Montreal. Two separate social notes in the *Sherbrooke Daily Record* – one in January and the other in April – confirm she was studying at the college.

> KEITH: Recent arrivals: Miss Belle McLeod, from Macdonald College, in company with her father, Mr. John F. McLeod, from Bury. (*Sherbrooke Daily Record*, Jan. 6, 1911)

> BURY: The many friends of Miss Belle McLeod will regret to learn she is home from Macdonald College, ill at the home of her father, Mr. John F. McLeod. (*Sherbrooke Daily Record*, Apr. 25, 1911)

Postcard of Macdonald College Women's Residence, ca. 1910 (BANQ.qc.ca)

> **EDUCATIONAL PROPOSITION OF SIR WILLIAM MACDONALD**
>
> Board of Governors of McGill University Now Prepared to Provide at Macdonald College for Training of Teachers.

Founding of Macdonald College Teacher Training Program (*Quebec Chronicle*, Jan. 9, 1907)

It is interesting to note that Dorothy entered the College very soon after it opened its teacher training program in 1907. A new Women's Residence was constructed to accommodate the influx of female students.

At that time, there was a severe shortage of teachers, especially in rural areas of the province. In June 1911, the head of the Macdonald Teachers School issued an appeal and offered a teacher-in-training bursary of at least $50 to anyone who, upon graduation, would agree to teach for three years in a rural school. This represented a significant incentive, given that the normal monthly teacher's salary for a Macdonald graduate at that time was $22 per month.

> Editor of the Chronicle.
>
> Dear Sir: May I trouble you to kindly call the atention of your readers to the new Bursary regulation for students of Macdonald College School for Teachers?
>
> This regulation provides that Bursaries of at least $50 each shall be paid to teachers-in-training in the School for Teachers who agree to teach three years in some rural elementary school in the Province of Quebec.
>
> Last year Macdonald College could have accommodated a number of additional students in the elementary class of the School for Teachers and at the present time we have requests from a large number of school commissioners who desire trained teachers for rural elementary schools and are willing to pay a fair salary, and to whom we can be of no service as practically all of our available graduate have secured schools.
>
> In view of the pressing need for trained teachers in such schools and the opportunity for securing such training at a minimum cost, it is hoped that a large number of persons from rural districts will avail themselves of the advantages of the new regulation. All applications for admission should be addressed to Dr. G. W. Parmelee, secretary, Department of Public Instruction, Quebec, P. Q.
>
> Yours truly,
> S. B. SINCLAIR,
> Head of the School for Teachers.
> Macdonald College, June 30, 1911.

Macdonald College bursary offer for rural teachers (*Quebec Chronicle*, July 3, 1911)

One-room rural schoolhouse

Within months of her graduation from Macdonald College in the spring of 1911, Dorothy received her first teaching job. The *Record* reported on September 11 that she was teaching at the Murray District schoolhouse. This one-room school, located on Scotch Road, was one of several such rural country schools in the Bury area. A summary of the school's history, written by Mrs. Herbert Rowell, was published in the *Record* in 1977:

> Around the year 1860, it was decided to build a school in West Keith near Thomas Murray's [home]. A few years later, a wood shed was added. . . .

Ages [of students] ranged from 7 to 14. . . In 1926, the school was closed, the district annexed to Bury where the pupils were taken. Two years [later] the building was sold to the Municipality of Bury. It was used as a shed to store wooden winter road rollers. It later became very dilapidated and eventually fell down and the debris moved away. (*Sherbrooke Daily Record*, Apr. 26, 1977)

Murray District schoolhouse (courtesy of Serena Wintle)

Two of the key events noted above, namely the closing of the school and the sale of the schoolhouse, were duly noted in the local press at the time:

> At a meeting of the board held on March 13 last to the effect that the Keith school should be closed was rescinded, and it was decided to close the Murray school and convey the pupils to the intermediate school at Bury. (*Sherbrooke Daily Record*, Apr. 27, 1926)

> REAL ESTATE FOR SALE: THE MURRAY SCHOOL HOUSE AND THE HARDWOOD FLAT SCHOOLHOUSE For sale at public auction, by the Protestant School Board, Township of Bury, at the Town Hall, Bury, on Saturday, January 14th. (*Sherbrooke Daily Record*, Jan. 6, 1928)

> Two of the old district school houses, the Murray school house and the Hardwood Flat school house, were sold by auction, the former selling for $200 and the other for $75. (*Sherbrooke Daily Record*, Jan. 17, 1928)

Teaching in a one-room school house in those days involved much more than teaching. In addition to nourishing the children's minds with the 3 R's, teachers also had to warm the children's bodies by constantly stoking the fire in the little wood stove. Of course, it was essential that the school always had an adequate supply of wood.

> TENDERS: For the supply and delivery of furnace wood. 10 cords of 20 in. wood to the Murray District School. 10 cords of 20 in. wood to the Hardwood Flat School. All wood to be sound body wood of either Beech, Birch or Maple. For the district schools, the price shall include piling in the shed in the summer. Tenders to be at my office not later than 2 o'clock pm Saturday, December 11th. (*Sherbrooke Daily Record*, Dec. 10, 1926)

Dorothy taught at the little Murray District School for only one year. However, the experience obviously left an impression on her, judging by the subject of her recitation at a Christmas party shortly afterwards:

> The Bury Methodist Sunday School held their annual Christmas Eve party and entertainment on December 24 in the Bury Town Hall. . . Miss Dorothy McLeod [performed] a recitation entitled "The Old School House." (*Sherbrooke Daily Record*, Dec. 28, 1912)

Big city school in Montreal

Then it was time for Dorothy to move on to new challenges in her teaching career. The move was a big one – from a tiny country school to a huge city school. It is not known how many years she taught in Montreal. Her obituary says "[She] taught in Aberdeen School in Montreal for a few years." However, we do know from the local papers' social notes that she began teaching there in the 1912-1913 school year and was still teaching there in December 1916:

> DEPARTURES: Miss Dorothy McLeod, to her school in Montreal . . . after the holidays with her parents, Mr. and Mrs. John F. McLeod. (*Sherbrooke Daily Record*, Jan. 11, 1913)

> Miss Belle McLeod, teacher in Montreal, has come to spend her holidays with her father. (*La Tribune*, July 12, 1916, translated by author)

> Miss Dorothy McLeod, teacher, of Montreal, is spending the holidays with her parents here. (*Sherbrooke Daily Record*, Dec. 28, 1916)

Aberdeen School was a large elementary school in downtown Montreal with an enrollment of approximately 1500 students. When Dorothy arrived there in September 1912, she had little idea of what she was about to experience a few months later. A *Montreal Gazette* article titled "Strikes are old-school in Quebec" by Roderick MacLeod and Mary Anne Poutanen tells the story of the Aberdeen Children's School Strike of 1913:

> Hundreds of Jewish students at Aberdeen elementary school on St. Denis St. went on strike in February 1913 over an offensive remark made by a

Aberdeen School, Montreal (BANQ.qc.ca; Album Massicotte 2734040)

Protestant teacher. In those days, Protestant schools accommodated most Jewish children, not always comfortably or respectfully. News of the strike travelled quickly in crowded classrooms, down alleys and over backyard fences. The incident came in the wake of mounting ethnic tension within Quebec society in general and the school system in particular. Students responded in part because most of them were from working-class families that had recently been involved in a violent labour strike, and they understood the mechanics of the strike as a tool to fight injustice. They set up strike headquarters in Carré St. Louis, where they created a strike committee, arranged picket duty and deemed anyone who went back to class a "scab." Delegations marched to the offices of the Yiddish-language newspaper the *Keneder Adler*, and to the Baron de Hirsch Institute community centre, seeking support for their cause. (*Montreal Gazette*, May 29, 2012)

Further details of this remarkable elementary student uprising are provided by the Museum of Jewish Montreal:

On February 28, 1913, as many as 500 Jewish students at Aberdeen School walked out of their classrooms as part of a general strike. What incited the rebellion and swift organization of children no older than age twelve? The previous day, a grade six teacher – one Miss McKinley – told her pupils that the increasing "dirtiness" of Aberdeen School coincided with a growing number of Jewish students. That same day, five students from her class – Moses Margolis, Joe Orenstein, Frank Sherman, Harry Singer, and Moses Skibelsky – met to discuss and plan a response to her comments.

After unsuccessfully demanding an apology from their teacher, the boys led their peers in a strike that commenced the following morning. Setting up headquarters in Saint Louis Square (across the street from their school on St. Denis), they quickly formed a strike committee. The strike leaders instructed the other children to maintain their ranks; any student who returned to school pre-emptively would be considered a scab. Their list of demands was short: the teacher ought to be transferred to another school.

Aberdeen School strike: children picketing, Feb. 28, 1913 (Jewish Public Library)

Aberdeen School, which had a large majority of Jewish students but was part of the Protestant school system, was filled with working-class children: even for the very youngest of the protestors, the organization and ethics of striking seemed to come intuitively. Indeed, the children had many role models, particularly from the massive garment workers' strike of 1912. Over the course of the day, the students picketed the school, marched to the offices of the *Keneder Adler* to give an interview, and went to the Baron de Hirsch Institute in pursuit of (adult) representation.

Rabbi Herman Abramowitz of Congregation Shaar Hashomayim and lawyer S. W. Jacobs acted as envoys for the children, meeting with the school's principal. Declining to comment publicly on the strike, the principal deferred the matter to school commissioners. Meanwhile, Miss McKinley offered a retraction of sorts: she claimed to regret having made comments that were "misunderstood by the children." Though this was not considered a sufficient apology, the strike committee agreed to return to school on Monday, allowing their adult representatives to finesse negotiations. The teacher was eventually transferred to another class, and commissioners made a point of hiring some Jewish teachers the following year, a long-standing demand of the Jewish community that the Protestant School Board had been loath to satisfy. It would take years, though, for larger numbers of Jewish teachers to be hired. (reference: http://imjm.ca/location/1382)

My image of Dorothy, as a teacher who taught with love, contrasted sharply with memories of my own primary school teacher, Louisa Elliott, who taught **without** much apparent love. How ironic it was that Dorothy and Louisa died within days of each other, as recorded in my late wife's diary.

Dorothy French death and Louisa Elliott funeral noted (Becky Fraser diary, May 23, 1970)

Business Career

It was probably around 1918 that Dorothy transitioned from education to business. Her obituary simply states "She later worked in the office of Belding-Corticelli in Montreal." Belding-Corticelli was an American textile company with several offices in Canada, including one in Montreal. It is not known exactly what Dorothy's position was, but other evidence suggests that she was perhaps a stenographer.

It is possible that Dorothy, together with some friends and/or business colleagues, established their own enterprise under the name of Clarke Helme Loomis, Limited. The Quebec Gazette lists Dorothy Isabella MacLeod as one of the principals of a company in the field of "general

Vintage Belding-Corticelli Canada ad (vieillespubs.com)

sales counselling." Unless the Dorothy mentioned was an imposter with an identical name, it seems that our Dorothy was indeed an entrepreneur.

Return to Cookshire

Following her father's passing in 1928, Dorothy returned to Cookshire to care for her mother. She soon became involved in various church and community organizations and was known for her recitations of prose and poetry at their meetings. A few examples of her activities:

> **" Clarke Helme Loomis, Limited "**.
>
> Public notice is hereby given that, under the Quebec Companies' Act, letters patent have been issued by the Lieutenant-Governor of the Province of Quebec, bearing date the second day of June, 1919, incorporating : Sarah Miller, Dorothy-Isabella MacLeod, Frances-Katherine LeSauteur, stenographers, Philip Presner and Adolphe Gardner, students at law, all of the city and district of Montreal, for the following purposes :
>
> To carry on a general sales counselling business comprising business analysis, business organization, business promotion, sales plans, advertising, and such other business reasonably incidental thereto ;

Dorothy Isabella MacLeod letters patent, Clarke Helme Loomis, Ltd. (*Quebec Gazette*, June 21, 1919)

- Women's Institute: appointed librarian (*Sherbrooke Daily Record*, Dec. 12, 1929)
- WCTU meeting: gave a reading of "The Land of Beginning Again" by Louisa Fletcher (*Sherbrooke Daily Record*, May 20, 1930)

> **The Land of Beginning Again**   **Louisa Fletcher**
>
> I wish that there were some wonderful place
> Called the land of Beginning Again,
> Where all our mistakes and all our heartaches
> And all of our poor selfish grief
> Could be dropped like a shabby old coat at the door,
> And never put on again.
>
> I wish we could come on it all unaware,
> Like the hunter who finds a lost trail;
> And I wish that the one whom our blindness had done
> The greatest injustice of all
> Could be at the gates like an old friend that waits
> For the comrade he's gladdest to hail.
>
> We would find all the things we intended to do
> But forgot, and remembered too late,
> Little praises unspoken, little promises broken,
> And all of the thousand and one
> Little duties neglected that might have perfected
> The day for one less fortunate.

"The Land of Beginning Again" (rainydaypoems.com)

> # The Revenge: A Ballad of the Fleet
>
> At Flores in the Azores Sir Richard Grenville lay,
> And a pinnace, like a fluttered bird, came flying from far away:
> "Spanish ships of war at sea! we have sighted fifty-three!"
> Then sware Lord Thomas Howard: "'Fore God I am no coward;
> But I cannot meet them here, for my ships are out of gear,
> And the half my men are sick. I must fly, but follow quick.
> We are six ships of the line; can we fight with fifty-three?"

"The Revenge: A Ballad of the Fleet," verse 1 (bartleby.com)

- Y.P.S. meeting: gave a reading of "The Revenge" by Tennyson (*Sherbrooke Daily Record*, Jan. 29, 1931)
- United Church Ladies Aid meeting: acted in a play (*Sherbrooke Daily Record*, June 15, 1932)
- Women's Institute meeting: gave readings from Dickens (*Sherbrooke Daily Record*, Apr. 25, 1934)

After her mother's death in 1933, Dorothy briefly returned to teaching, holding a position on the staff of Cookshire High School. The *Sherbrooke Record* noted her class's participation in the school's end-of-year event for parents and friends:

Cookshire Academy and classes, ca. 1910 (Fraser family archives)

Dearly beloved

The pupils of grade four and five of the Cookshire High School, in charge of Miss Dorothy MacLeod, gave an interesting recital of their English prose and poetry which they took in their year's work. (*Sherbrooke Daily Record*, June 15, 1934)

Dorothy MacLeod's career had now come full circle – from teacher to businesswoman to caregiver to teacher!

Chapter 5
Love and Marriage

Love and marriage, love and marriage
They go together like a horse and carriage
This I tell you, brother
You can't have one without the other.
– Sammy Cahn; popularized by Frank Sinatra

Horse and carriage (istockphoto; credit Larysa Marchenko)

I must confess I have very little hard information about the courtship of John and Dorothy. No personal diaries and no love letters have been discovered. Not even any overt suggestions of a budding romance in the Social Notes columns of the *Sherbrooke Daily Record*.

Courtship

Nonetheless, there is significant circumstantial evidence to indicate that this eventual couple knew each other from a young age and developed a mutual attraction as time went on. First of all, they were born in neighbouring villages of Lingwick Township. John was born in Scotstown in 1888. Three years later, Dorothy first saw the light of day in Gould, a scant seven miles away. Their respective families undoubtedly knew each other. Although they attended

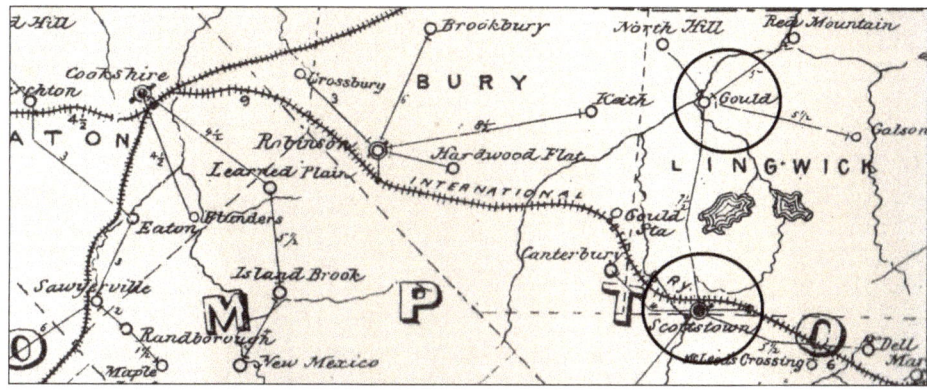

1896 map of Eaton, Bury and Lingwick townships, with Gould and Scotstown circled (*History of Compton County*)

different schools (John at Scotstown Academy and Dorothy at Bury Academy), they possibly attended common social events.

> Mr. John W. French has returned from a short trip to Montreal.
>
> Miss Dorothy MacLeod, of Montreal, spent a few days recently with her parents, Mr. and Mrs. John F. MacLeod.

John French and Dorothy MacLeod mentioned in consecutive paragraphs (*Sherbrooke Daily Record*, Dec. 11, 1923)

The first recorded hint of a possible relationship appeared in the *Record*'s Cookshire social notes column of December 11, 1923, when they were both working in Montreal. In this brief item, John and Dorothy were mentioned in consecutive paragraphs.

On September 9, 1924, the *Record* reported that John had attended the Scotstown Fair with Dorothy's mother (Mrs. John F. McLeod) and sister (Mrs. Harry Shirreffs). One can only conjecture that the reason Dorothy wasn't with them was because she was working in Montreal. There was a further indication of the close relationship between John's and Dorothy's families in 1928 when John was one of the pall bearers at Dorothy's father's funeral.

A family photo taken in the summer of 1934 (almost a year before she married

Family grouping including Annie French (left), John Wellington French (right), Aunt Lottie French & Aunt Dorothy MacLeod (back), Mackenzie children & Wickenden children. 1934

John French and Dorothy MacLeod with John's sisters and nieces in Cookshire, 1934 (courtesy of Ken Watson)

John) identifies Dorothy as "Aunt Dorothy MacLeod," indicating that she had already become a bona fide member of the French family.

By November, the relationship was obviously in full bloom as John and Dorothy were guests at a dancing party in Gould. It goes without saying, that for John, Dorothy was the Belle of the ball!

> GOULD: Mr. Malcolm A. MacDonald entertained a large gathering of friends very pleasantly at his home at North Hill when cards were played at several tables, and dancing was enjoyed in the spacious rooms when excellent music was furnished by Messrs. Arnold MacDonald, Gerald McKay and Artie Beaton. Out-of-town guests included Mr. John French and Misses Dorothy McLeod and Mary Morrison, of Cookshire, and Mr. and Mrs. Vernon Mayhew, their daughters, Alberta and Ethel, and son, Donald of Sherbrooke. At the close of the enjoyable evening, delicious refreshments were served by some of the ladies present. (*Sherbrooke Daily Record*, Nov. 20, 1934)

Given the fact that John and Dorothy had known each other for several years, one wonders why they waited so long before getting married. Some of their nieces share their speculations on this very personal question.

> When Grammy French [John's mother] died, I imagine that there was pressure for him to "find" a wife. I think Dorothy was the perfect choice. (Martha Wickenden MacKellar)

> I gleaned that Aunt Dorothy was in the wings for years, waiting for Uncle John to be free to marry her. He lived with my Grandmother French. But that is hearsay only. (Alice Wickenden MacEwen)

> Uncle John and Aunt Dorothy seemed to "hit it off" pretty well. (Don French)

Whatever the reason, they finally said "I do" on March 12, 1935, in New York City. Why in NYC? Niece Martha explains:

> They were married in New York because [Dorothy's sister] Eva Shirreffs and family lived there. I daresay it added to the excitement of their tying the knot, at last. (Martha Wickenden MacKellar)

The wedding

The wedding itself was rather unique in several respects. To begin with, it took place far away from home – in New York City, no less. This can be explained, perhaps, because Dorothy's sister lived there. The ceremony was performed in a private residence on a Tuesday, whereas Christian weddings are traditionally held in a church on a Saturday. And there were no guests present apart from the bride and groom, their two attendants and the minister. Upon reflection, I should not be

John and Dorothy wedding portrait (Malcolm Fraser collection)

Eva and Harry Shirreffs home in Bronxville, N. Y.; the living room (trulia.com)

surprised by this last characteristic because my own parents had an identically sized entourage at their exchange of vows in Cookshire in 1933. The marriage ceremony took place in the living room of Harry and Eva Shirreffs' home on Cassilis Avenue in the upscale Armour Villa neighborhood of Bronxville, N. Y., only about a mile from the Kennedy family compound on Pondfield Road.

> **MARRIAGES**
> FRENCH-MacLEOD—At the residence of Mr. and Mrs. H. W. Shirreffs, 108 Cassilis avenue, Bronxville, N. Y., on Tuesday, March 12th, at 4 p.m, by the Rev. M. F. Johnston, D.D., John Wellington French, son of the late Mr. and Mrs. C. W. B. French, to Dorothy Isabelle MacLeod, daughter of the late Mr. and Mrs. John F. MacLeod. Both of Cookshire, Que.

> **FRENCH—MacLEOD**
> Miss Dorothy Isabelle MacLeod and John Wellington French were married Tuesday, March 12, at the home of Mr. and Mrs. Harry W. Shirreffs on Cassilis Avenue.
> The Rev. M. F. Johnson, pastor of the Morisianna Presbyterian Church of New York City, performed the ceremony. Mrs. Shirreffs was matron of honor and Mr. Shirreffs was best man.
> Mr. and Mrs. French left for a wedding trip to Atlantic City and will remain there until the first of April when they will return to Cookshire, Canada, where they will make their home.
> Mrs. French has been visiting with Mr. and Mrs. Shirreffs since November.

John French and Dorothy MacLeod marriage announcements (above: *Sherbrooke Daily Record*, Mar. 15, 1935; right: *Bronxville Press*, Mar. 22, 1935)

Marriage announcement

Something else that struck me as unusual was the content of the wedding announcement notices in the newspapers. The write-up in the *Bronxville* (N. Y.) *Press* provided the basic facts and nothing more. The puny piece in the *Sherbrooke Daily Record* was even more barebones. Maybe it is because I was married in a different era, that I expected to see a more detailed description of the big event. You know – like a fashion editor's elaborate essay on the intricacies of the bride's gown, the jewellery she wore and her going-away outfit. To illustrate the point, here are excerpts from the published reports of two other weddings – that of Dorothy's sister, Eva, in 1915 and that of my own in 1968:

> The bride, who was given away by her father, looked charming in a white satin gown with tulle veil and orange blossoms, and carried a bouquet of white roses and lilies of the valley, her only ornament being a sapphire and diamond pendant, the gift of the groom. She was attended by her sister Dorothy, who was becomingly attired in pale pink crepe de chine and carried pink roses. (*Sherbrooke Daily Record*, Sep. 8, 1915)

> The bride, given in marriage by her father, wore an original gown of white peau de soie lined with corded silk, having a bodice of Italian lace with a round neckline buttoning down the back and long sleeves which were edged with white mink. The floor length skirt, cut on straight lines,

featured a cathedral length train caught at the back of the empire waistline accented with mink at the front. The train was edged with lace and had applique lace, both with pearls. A wedding band circlet of mink, encircled with crystals held in place her three quarter length veil of nylon illusion and she carried a cascade bouquet of Christmas red roses and miniature white carnations. Her jewelry was a single strand of pearls, a gift of the groom. (*Sherbrooke Daily Record,* Jan. 23, 1968)

In order to "dress up" John's and Dorothy's mediocre marriage memoir, I commissioned UK-based professional dress historian Jayne Shrimpton to compose a description that does justice to the attire of the bridal couple. Based solely on their wedding portrait, here is Jayne's write-up:

> This is a relatively unusual wedding photograph portraying your godparents, John and Dorothy, who married in 1935 in Dorothy's sister's home. You have advised that the location was Bronxville, a desirable and expensive suburb of New York City. Internet research reveals this to have been an exclusive, village-like residential area, shaped by cutting-edge architectural trends, and this seems to be reflected in the stylish interior of this modern room setting.
>
> Coming from rural Quebec, no doubt the couple found the sophisticated Bronxville milieu very different to that with which they were accustomed. Nonetheless, they evidently rose to the occasion for their intimate marriage ceremony in dress that was appropriately formal (smart and 'dressy') but discreet and elegant, in keeping with their age, both in their 40s. I am not aware of the time of day that the wedding actually occurred, but their appearance would broadly reflect a special afternoon or relatively relaxed evening event.
>
> John wears a smart tailored sack/sac suit – a regular type of office or 'Sunday best' day suit – not, for example, an evening tail coat or tuxedo. The three-piece style is conservative and traditional, comprising matching jacket, vest and trousers, the loose cut typical of the 1930s, but not displaying any extreme or high-fashion tailoring features such as pin-striped material or wide, sharp lapels. His classic white shirt may have a slightly starched collar and his modest knotted necktie – usually silk at that date – features small repeating motifs, a 'safe' choice. His appearance is conventional and respectable, a serious air also imparted by his steel-rimmed spectacles fashioned in the prevailing style.
>
> Ladies' flowing ankle- or floor-length gowns in softly-draping fabrics were favoured for special and semi-formal occasions during the 1930s, worn in certain afternoon and evening circumstances, both in public and at home. Dorothy has chosen a long, elegant black or dark-coloured velvet dress of slender cut, displaying an interesting yet modest neckline and long sleeves. It also features a narrow waist cord or belt and together these features express the prevailing vogue for a clinging medieval-inspired silhouette that was partly influenced by historical Hollywood costume dramas of the period.

Her hair, seemingly worn long in the traditional style, is drawn back into an unseen chignon or bun behind her head. The pale, shining object at her neck is a dress clip, perhaps of metal and/or glittering diamanté design: fashionable in the 1920s/1930s, dress clips sometimes held fabric together or, as here, were worn as a striking piece of jewelry. As a more overtly formal accessory – in this case bridal – Dorothy also wears a bodice corsage above her waist, the long, slanting shape also of fashionable 1930s style. It resembles flowers or petals but seems to be made from ribbons and bows. She and John look suitably well-dressed and attractive for their special day: they follow contemporary style but nothing is garish or ultra-glamorous: theirs is a carefully-chosen, conventional and restrained image. (Jayne Shrimpton)

The honeymoon

We know from one of the marriage announcements that John and Dorothy left for a 2-½ -week wedding trip to Atlantic City, New Jersey. No doubt they had lots of

Atlantic City postcard, 1935 (duftopia.com)

Atlantic City 1935 postmark (duftopia.com; retouched by Greg Beck)

time to see all the sights of this popular honeymoon destination and to send a "Having a wonderful time. Don't wish you were here!" postcard to the folks back home!

Thus marked the beginning of what would become a lifelong love story.

To borrow a 300-year-old expression: "And they lived happily ever after."

Chapter 6
Uncle John and Aunt Dorothy

Aunt is like a big mother and Uncle is like a big father. A best friend of our life.
– thebrandboy.com

Martha Louise Wickenden, Aunt Dorothy French, Harriet French Wickenden with Lady (dog)

Dorothy French with nieces Martha and Harriet Wickenden (courtesy of Ken Watson)

Harriet French Wickenden, John French, Rhona Mackenzie, Jocelyn Anne Wickenden, Martha Louise Wickenden, & Catherine Jean Wickenden - Cookshire, 1934

John French with Wickenden and Mackenzie nieces, 1934 (courtesy of Ken Watson)

Regardless of all they had achieved in their lives, John and Dorothy were, to their nieces and nephews, simply "Uncle John" and "Aunt Dorothy." And, I hasten to add, they were greatly loved by them. A letter from their 7-year-old niece, Alice, illustrates the extent of that love – the note ends with 30 hugs and 53 kisses!

That letter is one of several that Alice shared with me – correspondence that reflected the close relationship that she and her siblings had with their Uncle John and Aunt Dorothy.

Alice and John, ca. 1940 (courtesy of Alice Wickenden MacEwen and John French Wickenden)

Personal memories

In this chapter, we present a compilation of the first hand recollections of those who knew John and Dorothy best – their family. The mountain of memories – some going back more than 80 years – has been shared by the couple's nieces and nephews, grandnieces and grandnephews, most of whom were young children at the time. Now many of them are septuagenarians, octogenarians and nonagenarians. As seen through their young eyes, Uncle John and Aunt Dorothy take on special personae that complement the personalities portrayed in the preceding chapters. So, without further ado, to

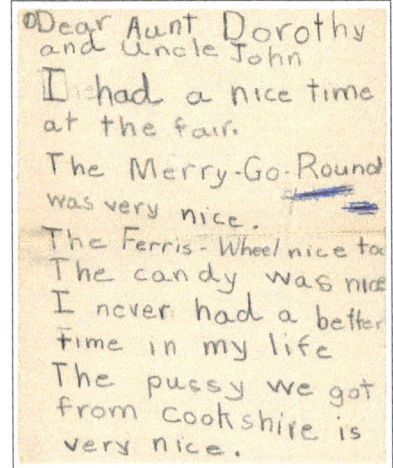
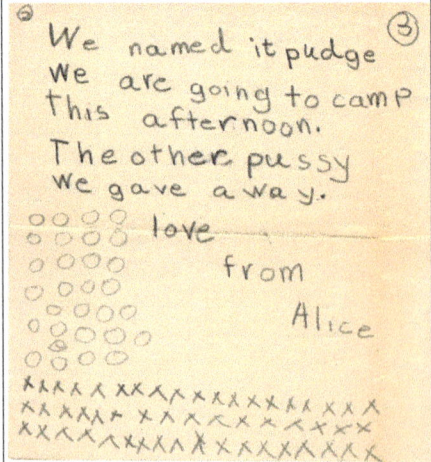

Letter from Alice to Uncle John and Aunt Dorothy (courtesy of Alice Wickenden MacEwen)

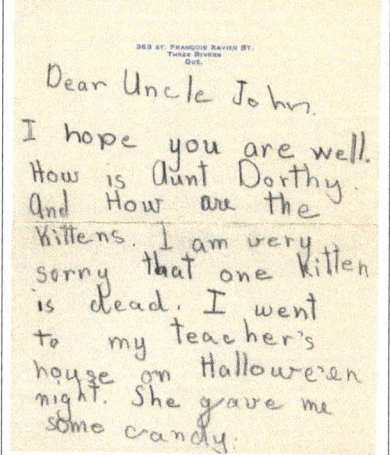 

Letter from Alice and Harriet to Uncle John, undated (courtesy of Alice Wickenden MacEwen)

 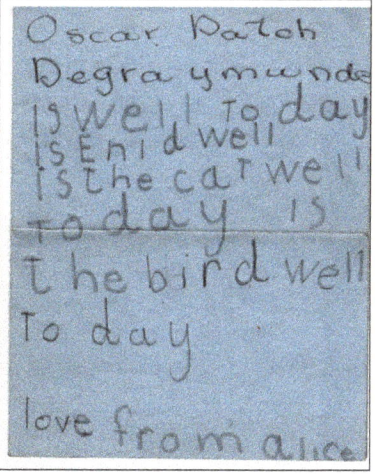

Letter from Alice to Uncle John and Aunt Dorothy, undated (courtesy of Alice Wickenden MacEwen)

them I pass my pen for their panoply of perspectives – sometimes forthright, often funny and always fond.

The following personal vignettes paint a picture how their family saw Uncle John and Aunt Dorothy:

> Going back as far as I can, my first memory of relatives was Uncle John. So he was number one. I was born in 1937, so those were the war years. He came to visit us in Three Rivers twice I believe, and always let me honk the horn just a few times. Gave me a nickel or two. Always encouraging me. Called my mother "Chief." He couldn't come more often because tires were scarce [during the War]; I sort of accepted that but

did not understand. We also visited them in Cookshire and it would have been at the Cookshire Fair time. It was special for us kids to go but, at my tender age, I don't remember much. I do recall staying with Uncle John and Aunt Dorothy at the [Main Street] house on the corner. (John French Wickenden)

Uncle John had a big heart, was kind, loving and encompassing. (Alice Wickenden MacEwen)

I have warm, fuzzy feelings about Uncle John and Aunt Dorothy. They were very close to their nieces and nephews, and then their grandnieces and grandnephews, especially since they didn't have children of their own. That is why I have so many photos of them during my childhood and teenage years. I remember they both came to my graduation from Bishop's University in 1968. (Leslie Buckle)

I thought of John and Dorothy as very kind and helpful – we enjoyed quite long talks and discussions, and they ensured that I visited as many places around about that would give me a good idea of the area and of my heritage. John took me to the cemetery to the graves of my grandfather and many other relatives, including his brother Charles (and Emily). He also took me to St. Peter's Church to see the window in memory of Horace Hall French and Harriet Bixby Ward, my grandfather's parents. One afternoon John organized a taxi, and we were a "jolly" party of John and Dorothy, Lottie and Malcolm and myself, taken on a drive around Lake Megantic, Scotstown (where the French family at one time owned a hotel) and other places of interest. I noted that a delay occurred when we had a puncture! We were at Lottie's for two evening meals, and I noted that John gave us much pleasure reciting some poetry. (Roger Lancey)

Uncle John was Mum's [Jocelyn's] favourite uncle, at least on the French side. If I'm not mistaken, she said he was gentle, had a lovely sense of humour, and that he understood children. (Mary Watson)

One time, it must have been in '43 or '44, when Maurice Richard began playing with les Canadiens, Uncle John asked me what I thought of the Rocket. I had no idea who he was, but Uncle John was quite excited and said, "Ooh, he's going to be a dandy, John-boy." Years later, after the Rocket retired in 1960, I played in a hockey league in Montreal North and Maurice was the referee. I played in that league for part of two winters before going north to work. Uncle John would have liked that! He certainly recognized a good one – before TV. (John French Wickenden)

He had banties, he had kittens and cats. We children in Trois Rivières named one of our cats

Maurice Richard memorial poster at Bell Centre, Montreal, 2000 (photo by author)

after his Patch. Maybe all his cats were Patch. The dog was Goldie and the horse was Queenie – wondrous names to me. Oh, and there were always canaries in a cage. (Alice Wickenden MacEwen)

I was always fascinated with Uncle John's suitcase when he came to visit – he called it his "grip" (or possibly spelled "grippe"). (Martha Wickenden MacKellar)

He wore black lace-up boots, which fascinated me. (Alice Wickenden MacEwen)

Above: Jocelyn and Martha Wickenden with Queenie in Cookshire, 1934; right: Martha on Queenie in Cookshire, 1932 (both courtesy of Martha Wickenden MacKellar)

Martha Louise Wickenden. Fall 1932

We knew Uncle John as a kind and caring person. I suspect, that as a young man, he might have been a go-getter, not afraid to try something different. (John French Wickenden)

Uncle John was a very kind man. Hard working, loving, and good to one and all, his family and his community. He gave of himself. (Alice Wickenden MacEwen)

Vintage grip bag (etsy.com)

Uncle John had what were called "spells." And also problems with his narrow esophagus. He would go to the Lahey Clinic [in Boston] for treatment. (Martha Wickenden MacKellar)

Destination Cookshire

A paragraph in John French's obituary mentions John and Dorothy's fondness of children and the visits of their nieces and nephews to Cookshire:

There were no children from this marriage, but they were both very fond of children, and several nieces and nephews enjoyed visiting at their home and were very happy in their company. (John W. French obituary)

The road to Cookshire, ca. 1960 (photo by author)

This section documents newspaper references to such visits and the memories of those making the journeys to the town where their Uncle John and Aunt Dorothy spent their entire married life.

> The Misses Jean, Jocqueline *(sic)* and Martha Wickenden have returned to their home in Montreal, after spending some time as guests of Mr. and Mrs. John W. French (*Sherbrooke Daily Record*, Sep. 10, 1937)

> Miss Harriette *(sic)* Wickenden, of Three Rivers, and Miss Margaret Mackenzie, of Montreal, are guests of Mr. and Mrs. John French. *(Note by Harriet: That was when my parents and three older sisters went to the world's fair in New York!)* (*Sherbrooke Daily Record*, Aug. 29, 1939)

> The Misses Jean, Jocelyn and Martha Wickenden have returned to Three Rivers after visiting Mr. and Mrs. John French. (*Sherbrooke Daily Record*, Aug. 29, 1939)

> Miss Dorothy Sheriffs, of Bronxville, N.Y., Miss Harriette Wickenden, of Three Rivers, and Miss Margaret Mackenzie, of Montreal, are guests of Mr. and Mrs. John French. (*Sherbrooke Daily Record*, Aug. 29, 1939)

> I have several memories of Cookshire and all that it meant to me. They go back to possibly the summer before my grandmother French died, then the winter following her death and a trip to Cookshire by train with my mother. I recall Arrowroot biscuits being offered, finally the Cookshire Station with Uncle John there and a horse and sleigh to carry us up the hill to their house – at that time at the turn of the road just

Harriet French Wickenden, Jocelyn Anne Wickenden, Mac French, Martha Louise Wickenden, Catherine Jean Wickenden, Rod French, John French Wickenden (Alice Mary Wickenden behind Martha).

Wickenden and French cousins (courtesy of Ken Watson)

next to the United Church. It was all magical to this little girl. (Martha Wickenden MacKellar)

Driving through Sherbrooke to Lennoxville and Mecca, Cookshire, next, we drove by a white building, CARNATION, THE HOME OF CONTENTED COWS. "And why not contented?" I thought, "living in such a nice sort of barn." (Alice Wickenden MacEwen)

When we drove from Lennoxville to Cookshire, "Almost there!," Dad stopped the car for Mother and we marveled at her special Eastern Townships place, THE HEIGHT OF LAND. (Alice Wickenden MacEwen)

Author's note: Me too! I marvel at that same amazing spot where you can see the distant mountain peaks in every direction.

On 11 July 1966 I took the 5 p.m. Dayliner train from Montreal West station on the lovely three-hour journey through the Eastern Townships countryside. John and Dorothy met me at the Cookshire train station, made

Carnation milk "from contented cows" (hodginshalls.hibid.com)

Carnation milk plant, Sherbrooke (laiteriesduquebec.com)

Twin Dayliners at Cookshire station, ca. 1962 (photo by author)

me immediately feel "at home," and indeed I was staying with them. (Roger Lancey)

I recall staying with Uncle John and Aunt Dorothy at the house on the corner. Uncle John always had butternuts and always hit his thumb cracking them! He would call me "John-boy." He had a cat called Patch, and the dog was Goldie, as I recall. He smoked a pipe, and had quite a few of them. (John French Wickenden)

There were new kittens to see, a dog was a constant, as was Billie the bird. (Alice Wickenden MacEwen)

We use to vacation at my Aunt and Uncle's house when I was very young. Eva Shirreffs [Aunt Dorothy's sister] was my grandmother. (Kathi Kressman)

Near Cookshire, height of land 360 degree views (photos by author, collage by Greg Beck)

Dearly beloved

American pavilion at Expo '67, Montreal, 1967
(photo by author)

I have fond memories of the only time we met Uncle John and Aunt Dorothy. Our family of four travelled east for Expo '67 and stayed with them for a few days in Cookshire. I recall one day going for a walk down a gravel road with my dad and Uncle John, which I think was near their home. I was – and still am – drawn to beautiful and unusual rocks. On this walk, I spotted a rock that I was convinced had gold in it. I distinctly recall Uncle John agreeing with me and vowing to take me to the jeweller's the next day to confirm it. AND HE DID! He seemed to know the jeweller and I was greatly saddened to learn it was fool's gold – which I had never heard of before. Nonetheless, it was a very special time and I loved them both instantly. (Margie French)

I only have the one memory of my Great-uncle John and Great-aunt Dorothy: when our family went to Expo '67 in Montreal in 1967. We stayed at their home for a couple of days, but I was only in Grade 2 at the time. Rod and Dorothy French also did the trip to Expo and I believe they stayed at John and Dorothy's home as well. That would have been the last time that any of the Frenches from out west would have seen them. (Donna Mikulecky)

They would pop in when they came to Three Rivers to our weddings. They would arrive in the house just as my mother was getting the bride and bridesmaids organized! It drove my mother mad. They seemed to have no idea that it WAS NOT THE RIGHT TIME TO POP IN! (Harriet Wickenden Taylor)

Uncle John the entertainer

Only in doing research for this book did I become aware of this surprising aspect of John French's personality. Up until then, I had always understood my godfather to have been a serious and reserved man.

> Uncle John was a man who could amuse children for hours. He charmed his nieces and nephews with his tricks and stories. He would take us out to the shed where there was always a bucket of butternuts. Holding a nut on a stump, he would hammer away at it and eventually – sometimes not soon enough – as we stood waiting, the fateful moment occurred when the hammer came down on Uncle John's thumb. The histrionics that followed were worthy of an Oscar! He jumped around,

Uncle John and Aunt Dorothy

Uncle John French & John French Wickenden

John Wellington French & Catherine Jean Wickenden. March 1927

Uncle John playing on grass with nephew John Wickenden; with niece Jean Wickenden in sled in 1927 (both courtesy of Ken Watson)

Jocelyn Anne Wickenden & Uncle John French. Cookshire, 1933

Above: Uncle John with nephews Roddy French and Mac French, 1935 (courtesy of Leslie Buckle)

Right: Uncle John with niece Jocelyn Wickenden on swing, Cookshire, 1933 (courtesy of Ken Watson)

moaned, groaned and we laughed and laughed. All the while, Aunt Dorothy smiled and got on with meal preparations. (Alice Wickenden MacEwen)

In 1939 my parents and three older siblings went to New York City to the World's Fair. I was deposited with Uncle John and Aunt Dorothy in Cookshire. Mostly I remember him telling me stories about "the bears of St. Germain." Whether they were fabricated or true, I've no idea! All this while in bed with him, while Aunt Dorothy busily prepared breakfast! That would be frowned on now, I expect. I recall going to pick up pies at someone's house, and to the Dew Drop Inn. It was sort of the hangout for gossip, and possibly the mail as well. (Harriet Wickenden Taylor)

I remember Aunt Dorothy and Uncle John as kind, cheerful and always happy to welcome us into the house in Cookshire. Uncle John was full of things to do, tricks to play, small adventures, candy, chocolate bars. (Alice Wickenden MacEwen)

"Oh Mama! My thumb! Oh Mama!" (sketch by James Harvey)

Uncle John and Aunt Dorothy

A specific memory I have is one time when my parents, brother, and I were visiting Uncle John and Aunt Dorothy, and Uncle John got out a BB gun, and allowed us to practice shooting at an aluminum foil pie plate that he attached to a post in the garden. It was so much fun! I spoke to my brother Ron about memories of Uncle John. He too remembered the BB gun story. He also remembered that Uncle John kept rabbits and that we were allowed to play with them. One day Uncle John took us for a ride (in his immaculate condition 1950s model royal blue car) out in the country, where we fished in a pond stocked with trout and Ron caught a big one. (Leslie Buckle)

I remember that Uncle John enjoyed the poems of William Henry Drummond (1854-1907) who, I just learned from Wikipedia, was a doctor who graduated from Bishop's University and taught there for some time. He wrote poems in French-Canadian dialect which were apparently very popular. Uncle John had memorized and would recite "Little Bateese." My father was so impressed he made a recording of it. (Leslie Buckle)

On the last evening of my visit to Cookshire in 1970, Uncle John performed his "finale" for us, reciting his masterpiece, the story of "Little Bateese." It was so good to hear this poem one last time. (Roger Lancey)

Little Bateese
By William Henry Drummond (1854–1907)

You bad leetle boy, not moche you care
How busy you're kipin' your poor gran' père
  Tryin' to stop you ev'ry day
  Chasin' de hen aroun' de hay—
  W'y don't you geev' dem a chance to lay?
    Leetle Bateese!

Off on de fiel' you foller de plough,
Den w'en you're tire you scare de cow,
  Sickin' de dog till dey jomp de wall,
  So de milk ain't good for not'ing at all—
  An' you're only five an' a half dis fall,
    Leetle Bateese!

Too sleepy for sayin' de prayer to night?
Never min', I s'pose it'll be all right.
  Say dem to-morrow—ah! dere he go!
  Fas' asleep in a minute or so—
  An' he'll stay lak dat till de rooster crow,
    Leetle Bateese!

Den wake us up right away tout de suite
Lookin' for somet'ing more to eat,
  Makin' me t'ink of dem long leg crane—
  Soon as dey swaller, dey start again;
  I wonder your stomach don't get no pain,
    Leetle Bateese!

But see heem now lyin' dere in bed,
Look at de arm onderneat' hees head;
  If he grow like dat till he's twenty year
  I bet he'll be stronger dan Louis Cyr,
  An' beat all de voyageurs leevin' here,
    Leetle Bateese!

Jus' feel de muscle along hees back,
Won't geev' heem moche bodder for carry pack
  On de long portage, any size canoe;
  Dere's not many t'ing dat boy won't do,
  For he's got double-joint on hees body too,
    Leetle Bateese!

But leetle Bateese! please don't forget
We rader you're stayin' de small boy yet;
  So chase de chicken an' mak' dem scare,
  An' do w'at you lak wit' your ole gran' père,
  For w'en you're beeg feller he won't be dere—
    Leetle Bateese!

"Little Bateese" (bartleby.com)

> The summer that I spent a week with Aunt Ellen, Uncle John took me for drives several afternoons. We never ran out of conversation. (Alice Wickenden MacEwen)

> Uncle John loved to sing, had a deep voice and he sang very loudly. "Lanctot Picatot Fiddle dee a mash a po, Lanctot Picatot Fiddle dee a mash a po." (John French Wickenden)

> Uncle John sang ditties, as I did at home with two parents who sang well and loved song. He never played any instrument for me – or, at least, not when I was around. (Alice Wickenden MacEwen)

It seems that John was a bit of a trickster, as indicated in the following anecdote recalled by one of his grandnephews:

> A vacuum cleaner salesman arrived at Uncle John and Aunt Dorothy's home, to demonstrate the latest in vacuum cleaners. Uncle John was in his bedroom where they had plugged in the vacuum, although the demonstration itself was being done in another room. Every time the salesman tried to demo a feature, Uncle John would unplug the vacuum until the sales guy finally gave up. I am not sure if he ever owned up to what he had done. (Ron Buckle)

Apparently John loved to sing hymns – and not only in Church. My dad often told us the story of one night long, long ago when he and John were both young and foolish. It seems that after drinking a little too much dandelion wine (or other such Prohibition-era homebrew), John was seen at midnight waltzing down Main Street in front of St. Peter's Church, belting out "Rock of Ages," "Abide With Me" and other favourites at the top of his lungs! It's kind of hard to imagine, but my dad didn't lie – even though he did occasionally stretch the truth!

Aunt Dorothy's humble hospitality

Based on the comments that follow, it is clear that Dorothy French's practice of hospitality should have qualified her as an Oscar candidate for Best Actor (we used to say "Best Actress") in a Supporting Role.

> Aunt Dorothy went along with the performances and entertainment with a gentle smile, but probably thinking at the same time, "HOW LONG, OH LORD, HOW LONG?" She fed us, patiently and well, and Uncle John provided Bull's Head ginger ale. Every year he brought us a whole case of it. (Alice Wickenden MacEwen)

> I never knew Aunt Dorothy other than in her role as the Aunt Dorothy of "Aunt Dorothy and Uncle John." When she married Uncle John, she took on his extended family, she was patient and loving and kind. Long-suffering might fit into the picture, too. (Alice Wickenden MacEwen)

> Dorothy was just "there," so to speak. Uncle John was the drawing card.

She got the meals, did the clearing up and the cleaning up, selfish little creature that I was! He was entertaining and doubtless more "fun" if that's the right word. But when you're six years old and getting ALL the attention, "what's not to like?" (Harriet Wickenden Taylor)

Vintage Bull's Head ginger ale bottles (bulls-head.com)

When I think of it, likely Aunt Dorothy's work was never done. Uncle John would have been lost without her. Dorothy just smiled and seemed content. (Martha Wickenden MacKellar)

I didn't appreciate at the time that Aunt Dorothy was always loyally in the background making the happy home life possible, meal after meal, bed after bed, for the children who visited them. (Alice Wickenden MacEwen)

Aunt Dorothy was a very kind lady. She made special meals for sure. Breakfast was stacks of toast made on a wood-burning stove, clean as a whistle, right on the steel. (John French Wickenden)

Aunt Dorothy was a loyal wife who took on Uncle John's family, always with a smile and an apron. He amused and she gave us a happy home to visit, time after time. (Alice Wickenden MacEwen)

Aunt Dorothy deserves top billing as well for her patience. I am sure there were times when my mother assumed that one or more of us would be welcome as visitors in Cookshire and could Dorothy refuse? It was heaven for us – more mouths for her to feed, likely some laundry to do as well. Just a thought – women understand these things. (Martha Wickenden MacKellar)

Aunt Dorothy was always there, always smiling and generous with her domestic skills. We chatted in the kitchen where she was lodged much of the time. I never gave her long hours given to Annie's children a second thought. At breakfast there were piles of buttered toast which, to me, was the food of the gods. (Alice Wickenden MacEwen)

I remember Dorothy whipping up a beautiful omelet for us in a cast iron frying pan. She finished the omelet in the oven and it came out high and delicious. (Muriel French Fitzsimmons)

Dearly beloved

I think it was the Summer of '42 or '43 that Uncle John worked as foreman in charge of a Shawinigan job for Dad. I cannot imagine that Dorothy was thrilled to be spending a summer away from Cookshire, but of course she had no choice. They lived in the vacated flat of one of the high school teachers. Was I "invited" to go and spend a few days with them?

So I enjoyed my time with Dorothy – managed to go to the "boating club" (NO boats) and got a bad sunburn. Another day Dorothy and I went to a movie, a matinee where "Fantasia" was playing. I had to TRY to look 16 in order to get in – remember wearing a reversible raincoat with light beige color exposed, and sunglasses to complete the disguise. We both enjoyed it – I doubt that Dorothy saw too many movies otherwise. She was a VERY patient woman and Uncle John was fortunate to have such a wife. (Martha Wickenden MacKellar)

Memories of Cookshire

Certain places in Cookshire have left indelible impressions on the memories of the Frenches' nieces and nephews:

At almost the tail end of my family of six, I missed out, I thought, on a lot of Cookshire time. The Dew Drop Inn was magic in name. (Alice Wickenden MacEwen)

I was at the Cookshire Fair at least twice when Uncle Charlie led the animals into the fairground ring. He led a brown bull or cow, what did I

Dew Drop Inn postcard, ca. 1935 (courtesy of Roger Dionne)

Cookshire Fair cattle parade, ca. 1960 (photos by author)

know? But I thought it most appropriate. He wore a brown suit and was stooped, to me the creature was of a similar posture. They were a match in brown. (Alice Wickenden MacEwen)

A big event for me was going in the car to the post office for the mail. (John French Wickenden)

Uncle John would take me to the post office sometimes. I was intrigued by the boxes, the system. We had postal delivery at the door in Trois-Rivières. We grew up calling the city Three Rivers. When I lived in Morrisburg, Ont., I always "went to get the mail." It was as much a meeting spot as had been my observation as a little girl at the post office in Cookshire. (Alice Wickenden MacEwen)

Folklore and foibles

Everyone carries with themselves through life their individual peculiarities of appearance, habit and expression. "Uncle John" was no different. It is in that context that the following conjectures and characteristics are lovingly shared.

Dearly beloved

Uncle John was always relaxed, and I used to wonder what he did. I believe he and Uncle Charlie worked on the railways through Ontario or further West in the summers, and made their money there. Then he invested wisely and so it went – I can only surmise. (John French Wickenden)

It was a rather on-going "joke" in the family as to where John got his money. We all knew how generous he was, but the source of that income seemed to be a mystery. It was assumed (with precious little actual evidence) that he had made money when young, perhaps had a shareholding portfolio or whatever. (Roger Lancey)

Author's note: Perhaps "Uncle John" was not the sole source of their apparent well-to-do-ness. Maybe "Aunt Dorothy" helped feather the family nest with a few flakes of gold!

Uncle John was as cross-eyed as a bear! His shins itched and he scratched them a lot – just like me now! He also talked very loudly on the telephone – especially when on long distance! (John French Wickenden) *Author's note: My folks also!*

John French walked pigeon-toed and I copied him as a young child and ended up walking the same way! (the late Mac Fraser, as told to his first wife, Janice, many years ago)

Author's note: For me it was John French's walking gait that fascinated me. From a standing position with both feet pointing straight ahead, John would lift his right foot and suddenly turn it 90 degrees to the right before placing it on the ground. Then the left foot would take a normal step forward. Meanwhile, the right foot would somehow return to the normal straight-ahead position in preparation for the next step. And the sequence would be repeated ad infinitum. I was able to copy it perfectly so my siblings would often ask me to "walk like John French!"

Uncle John's words of approval, or admiration, to children and maybe others were "NOW THAT'S A DANDY!"(Alice Wickenden MacEwen)

Author's note: When my late wife, Becky, and I visited John and Dorothy after John had just returned home from a stay in the Sherbrooke Hospital, he told us (in reference to Head Nurse Miss Frances Whittle) "She was a dandy!" After we left their house, Becky (who had worked as a nurse under Miss Whittle) said to me, "If only he knew the real Miss Whittle. She was always on the warpath, telling me my uniform was too short. She lived in the Stone Age; she wore hers three inches from the floor!"

Uncle John loved clocks. You always heard the chimes when visiting. (John French Wickenden)

Author's note: Moi aussi! When I had to choose my 25-years' service gift from IBM, I chose a beautiful German-made wall clock that chimed every quarter hour. But my dear late wife could not tolerate it, so I had to deactivate the musical mechanism.

Chapter 7
John W. French, MLA

A politician should have three hats. One for throwing into the ring, one for talking through, and one for pulling rabbits out of if elected. – Carl Sandberg

John Wellington French portrait (courtesy of Mary Watson)

Bright blue Conservative blood had already been flowing through John W. French's veins for 66 years when he took the profound plunge into active politics. Of course, as mentioned in Chapter 3, John had earlier dabbled in the political process but not to the same degree.

The nomination

John's nomination as the Union Nationale candidate for Compton County didn't just happen "out of the blue," so to speak. Rather, it was due to a confluence of circumstances. Firstly, there was the untimely passing of John's older brother Charles (better known as "C. D.") while still in office as MLA for Compton County and Minister of Mines in the Maurice Duplessis provincial government. Secondly, there was Duplessis's desire that an anglophone should be elected to replace the deceased Member. John's nomination was given prominence in the local press:

> With almost a single voice, the supporters of the National Union cause nominated John French, 66-year-old retired contractor of Cookshire as candidate in the September 15 by-election.
>
> Hon. J. D. Bégin [Minister of Colonization and chief organizer] lauded the desire of Prime Minister Maurice Duplessis to have an Anglo-Canadian as representative for Compton County, declaring that it represented the spirit of tolerance and respect for the minorities that featured the National Union. "When Mr. Duplessis goes to Ottawa, he can point to the manner in which Quebec respects the rights of the minorities and can justifiably demand that the federal government do the same."
>
> After thanking the convention for the honour bestowed upon him, Mr. French said that he had been reluctant to allow his name to stand before the convention but had done so at the personal request of the Prime

John W. French nomination (*Sherbrooke Daily Record,* Aug. 2, 1954)

Minister. "But now that I am nominated, I will be in the fight to win." (*Sherbrooke Daily Record,* Aug. 2, 1954)

Indeed, John was a reluctant candidate. In fact, he had attempted unsuccessfully to convince a good friend to stand for the nomination instead of himself:

My dad, E. Lionel Hurd (1907-2001), was a political animal and strong Tory (federal) and Union Nationale (Quebec) supporter. I recall my dad and Mr. John French discussing the [1954] nomination on the porch at the latter's Craig Street residence [in Cookshire] on a warm summer's evening. As I remember, Mr. John French asked my dad to stand for the nomination, but Dad declined because of his divorce from my mother. On the way home, Dad explained that Maurice Duplessis had arranged with the other parties to each run English-speaking candidates in Compton County. Dad felt that Duplessis needed the English content in the Quebec government. (Jim Hurd)

John French campaign event report (*Sherbrooke Daily Record*, Sep. 3, 1954)

John French campaign meetings schedule (*La Tribune*, Aug. 30, 1954)

The campaign

Almost from nomination day, John's election campaign got underway with English and French newspaper ads and a series of public events and personal visits across the county, from Saint Malo to Scotstown, East Angus to East Hereford and all points in between. The campaign was officially launched with a big kick-off rally in East Angus on September 2 where Premier Duplessis was the headline speaker.

A full-page newspaper ad, featuring Premier Duplessis boasting of all the benevolence bestowed on Compton County by his Union Nationale government and promising more of the same, appeared in the local papers.

In addition to the ambitious schedule of public "town halls," John and his team of volunteers were busy knocking on doors throughout the territory. Two of the people who received such electioneering visits recall their experiences:

> I was born in Galson between Scotstown and Megantic . . . My father was a farmer and a butcher . . . We moved to Scotstown where I attended school. My uncle was mixing cement by hand for the foundation of a new barn. When John French saw that when he came to visit, he arranged to immediately bring in a cement mixer to help out. (Erwin Watson)

John French campaign ad (*Sherbrooke Daily Record*, Sep. 15, 1954)

John came electioneering in Gould and entered our house by the front door to the parlour. He was the only person I ever knew to enter our house by the front door. (Clyne Macdonald)

On the eve of the election, the *Sherbrooke Daily Record* published an endorsement of John French's candidacy on its Editorial page. It stated:

John French is a lifelong and highly respected resident of the county, a man who is seeking office solely because he believes he is most capable of carrying out the enlightened policies which were effected by his brother . . . Mr. French is obviously the man most capable of assuring the future progress of Compton County . . .

The Compton County Vote

When the electors of Compton County go to the polls tomorrow, they should base their decision on two factors and two factors alone—the candidate and the record of the government.

The Union Nationale candidate, John French, is a lifelong and highly respected resident of the country, a man who is seeking office solely because he believes he is best capable of carrying out the enlightened policies which were effected by his brother, the late Mines Minister Charles French who represented the county at Quebec from 1946 until his death last spring.

Personally, and because of his close relations with the administration, Mr. French is obviously the man most capable of assuring the future progress of Compton County and is in the best position to complete those undertakings which had been instituted by the late Minister.

As for the record of the Government, Premier Duplessis and his ministers have done much for the province and for the county of Compton. Their works are there to speak for themselves.

The whole province of Quebec is prospering as it never prospered before. It is expanding in every direction. And the Government is making every effort to see that the public services keep pace with this economic expansion.

The Government can speak of a record of accomplishment. The Opposition can only offer promises that it has no chance of fulfilling for years to come.

These are the basic factors Compton County voters must take into consideration tomorrow.

John W. French endorsement editorial (*Sherbrooke Daily Record*, Sep. 14, 1954)

The campaign was not without some controversy. In a *Sherbrooke Daily Record* article under the headline "Missisquoi Member Claims Federal Interference In Compton Election", Jean-Jacques Bertrand alleged that a son of Prime Minister Louis St-Laurent [himself also a Compton County native] urged Compton voters to vote against the Union Nationale in the by-election. Apparently Mr. St-Laurent's son had told voters that his father had sent him a message to vote against John W. French, the Union Nationale candidate.

The victory

John French was elected with an overwhelming majority, obtaining 70 percent of the votes cast. In an address to the Victoria Hall crowd celebrating the victory, he spoke the following message:

John W. French election victory report (*Sherbrooke Daily Record*, Sep. 14, 1954)

Assemblée Nationale, Quebec City (photo by author)

It has pleased me very much to know that the people from my county have placed their confidence in me. We have had a fine clean campaign and I am grateful to all who helped me. I am truly convinced that Union Nationale is the best party . . . I appreciate the honour given me and will do my best to be worthy of it. (*Sherbrooke Daily Record*, Sep. 14, 1954)

Speaking in the Legislative Assembly

John French's first speech in Quebec's Legislative Assembly (now known as the National Assembly) in November 1954 was very noteworthy in two respects. First, he was accorded the singular honour of moving the adoption of the government's Throne Speech. Secondly, he delivered his speech in English. Following are excerpts from the official report of John's maiden speech in Quebec City:

> Address in response to the Throne Speech. Mr. French (Compton) rises. (Applause from the right).
>
> I move, seconded by the Member for Gatineau (Monsieur Desjardins), that the following address be presented to the Honourable Lieutenant-Governor of the province of Quebec. We, the members of the Legislative Assembly of Quebec, meeting in session, do sincerely extend, with the assurance of our loyalty to Her Majesty, our humble thanks for the speech that was delivered, in order to make known the reason for the convocation of the Chambers. Allow me to tell you how much I appreciate the honour given to my electors and to myself in asking me to move the traditional address in response to the Throne Speech. It is always a formidable task for a Member to deliver his maiden speech in the Chamber, and I am certain that it is even more so when his first speech is to move the adoption of such an important resolution.
>
> Before continuing, I am sure that you will understand if I pay homage to the memory of my dear brother, the late Honourable Charles D. French. My brother brought additions to the already impressive development of our natural resource wealth and contributed greatly to the boom in the province regarding the exploitation of our mineral riches. He was a good Canadian, a good citizen, and a very good representative of Compton, and I also believe, an excellent Minister of Mines. I know that he was proud to participate in the administration of the province under the Union Nationale, that he gave his full and loyal support to his leader, the Premier, who in the opinion of my brother and myself, is one of the most competent and constructive statesmen that Canada has ever produced.
>
> To my electors, I offer my thanks, recognizing that they elected me with the greatest majority in the history of Compton County. I recognize that this mark of confidence is a tribute to the services rendered by my brother and a testimony to the very significant confidence in the policies of the Premier and of the Union Nationale that have done so much for the province in general and for Compton County in particular. I intend to serve this mandate to the best of my ability. I wish to express not only

my personal gratitude but that of my fellow English-speaking citizens of Compton County, our recognition of the generosity shown by the majority, who under the enlightened leadership of the Premier, maintains minority representation in the public service. I am proud to say that no Quebec government has had more consideration for the rights of its English-speaking citizens, has taken more care to protect their interests than that of the current Premier and the Union Nationale. During these troubled times in which we live, a stable government that both preaches and practices policies of real stability is the very foundation of security. . .

The Premier of Quebec has undertaken very delicate negotiations with the Prime Minister of Canada several weeks ago. Here in Quebec, the vast majority of citizens know that our Premier will participate in the current negotiations in a spirit of justice and with a desire of cooperation, but at the same time, with unwavering vigour and a fearless devotion and without reproach toward the constitutional rights and interests of the province for which he is responsible. I would like to congratulate him and thank him for his unfailing devotion toward his compatriots and the citizens of the province, for the clear legislative program that he has submitted and at the same time for his stable and progress-generating policies. He can count on my friendship and loyal cooperation, on that of the citizens of Compton County in particular and at the same time, of the vast majority of the province. (Applause) (Debates of the Legislative Assembly – 24th Legislature — 3rd Session Vol. 1 – Nov. 1954 to Jan. 1955, translated by author)

The Quebec press reacted to John's opening speech, especially with respect to the fact he delivered it in English:

> Although Mr. French speaks French very well, he preferred to deliver his maiden speech in his mother tongue. (*Action Catholique*, Nov. 9, 1954, translated by author)

> This is the fourth time since 1867 that an English-speaking Member has moved the adoption of the Throne Speech. (*Chronicle Telegraph*, Nov. 19, 1954)

> Traditionally, it is an English-speaking Member who seconds the motion that was moved by a French-speaking Member. However, on only three occasions in the annals of parliamentary debates were there exceptions: in 1869, 1886 and 1894. (*L'Événement*, Nov. 19, 1954, translated by author)

An examination of the debates of the Legislative Assembly during the initial Session following John's election indicates that he was present for the majority of the votes taken. However, he did not often speak during the debates. Due to the unavailability of the debate records of subsequent Sessions during John's mandate, his speaking/voting record for those Sessions is unknown.

Caring for Compton

Unlike the uncertainty regarding his speaking record in Quebec City, there is little doubt about what he did for Compton County. During his 644 days as MLA, John French was always available and very dedicated to the needs of his constituents, whatever they were. In order to respond to the population's requests and concerns, he established regular office hours in the Government Building (i.e., the County Building) in Cookshire.

John French MLA office hours, Cookshire (*Sherbrooke Daily Record*, Sep. 20, 1954)

During his term as Member of the Quebec Legislative Assembly, John French was very busy representing his constituents in a wide variety of ways, including the initiation of projects and the support of municipalities and individuals. Following are several examples:

> Mr. L. J. Lane, chairman of the Cookshire Protestant School Board, has announced that the loan resolution in connection with the addition to, and renovation of, the present school building has been passed unanimously by the Central Board of Compton County and the Department of Education at Quebec. . . The final decision was to add a gymnasium ... and two additional classrooms ... [equipped with] the

Cookshire High School extension and new County Building, ca. 1960 (photo by author)

necessary science equipment... A grant of $52,825 has been pledged by the Provincial Government through the cooperation of John W. French, M.P.P. for Compton County. (*Sherbrooke Daily Record*, Feb. 15, 1956)

The construction of the new County Building was made possible thanks to a substantial grant obtained after much effort by the provincial Member for Compton County, Mr. John French. (*La Tribune*, Nov. 18, 1955, translated by author)

Grants Received By Bury Council

The Bury Council has announced that two substantial grants for much needed improvements have been received from the Provincial Government. As a result of these funds, secured through the efforts of John French, of Cookshire, M. L. A. for Compton, residents of the Lower Village will have town water, and through it, adequate protection from fire hazards, with a possible lowering of taxes. The other grant will be used for road work. (*Sherbrooke Daily Record*, Sep. 29, 1955)

Farm Forum Groups Oppose Exhibition Expropriation

A special resolution has been sent to John French, M. L. A. for Compton, from the members of the Cookshire Farm Forum in regards to the question of expropriation, on the part of the City of Sherbrooke, of the ETAA [Eastern Townships Agricultural Association] property... with a request that he use his influence to prevent such expropriation. (*Sherbrooke Daily Record*, Jan. 28, 1956)

I know that roads got paved and constituents were cared for if in need, financial, medical or in dire straits. (Alice Wickenden MacEwen)

COOKSHIRE: The annual banquet of the 4-H Calf Clubs was held here last night, terminating Achievement Day of the Island Brook and Sawyerville Club, which took place yesterday in conjunction with the Cookshire Fair... Seated at the head table were John French, M. L. A. for Compton, C. Bouchard, of the Federal Department of Agriculture, Walter Hodgman, secretary of the Compton County Agricultural Society [and others]. (*Sherbrooke Daily Record*, Aug. 16, 1955)

The secretary [of St. Peter's Church vestry] was instructed to write to J. W. French, M. L. A., expressing the thanks of the congregation and the provincial Roads Department for the paving of the driveway to the parish hall and the rectory garage. (*Sherbrooke Daily Record*, Feb. 1, 1955)

In the summer of 1955, between my second and third years at Bishop's, I was looking for a job. I remember as if it were yesterday: standing on the porch at John's house asking if there might be a job available at the provincial road department in Cookshire. (You may remember their office right on the corner across from the United Church). Surely enough,

I ended up with a job there in the surveying department working for Ken Flanders. It was a most enjoyable experience, surveying roads and drawing up plans to be used for road rebuilding. I have a recollection of him [John French] doing a very good job for his constituents, and that he was a well-respected Member of the provincial government. (Stanley Parker)

The fall from grace

Being a politician is a perilous and precarious profession – you are IN one day, OUT the next. John's term as an MLA ended with the call of a Quebec provincial general election for June 20, 1956. Although he ran for re-election, he was unsuccessful, losing to Liberal candidate Fabien Gagnon. My mom recorded the event in her diary most succinctly:

Duplessis campaign button, 1950s (blacklocks.ca)

> June 20, 1956: Went to vote. Poor John French is out. (Alice Fraser's diary)

So, for John and Dorothy, it meant returning to their retirement life in Cookshire and continuing to care for others, just like they had done for many years.

La Grande Noirceur

John French served under Maurice Duplessis during the latter years of the period in Quebec history that later became known as "La Grande Noirceur" ("The Great Darkness"). The Canadian Encyclopedia characterizes the era as follows:

> Maurice Duplessis, who was known as "le Chef," was Premier of the province [of Quebec] from 1936 to 1939 and again from 1944 to 1959. The leader of the conservative Union Nationale party, Duplessis ruled the province with an iron fist. The era eventually came to be known as La Grande Noirceur. Duplessis rewarded supporters with patronage and punished opponents with repression. (thecanadianencyclopedia.ca)

A 1999 National Post article summarizes the conclusions of a 1991 Royal Commission that examined the matter:

> In 1961, a royal commission, reviewing the Union Nationale record, estimated that kickbacks paid out by companies doing business with the provincial government over a 16-year period came to about $100-million, or more than a billion in today's bucks. . . . Tooling through the countryside during Duplessis' watch, you could always tell which riding

had voted for the Union Nationale, and which had sinned. The roads in Union Nationale ridings were paved, the others weren't. (*National Post*, June 12, 1999)

"Why does the pavement end here?" (sketch by James Harvey)

Personal anecdotes from that period shed additional light on that period of darkness:

> At the time, in the early 1950s, my dad was mayor of Newport Township and Hon. C. D. French was the Member for Compton County. One day, Mr. French stopped by and asked Dad if he could use a grant of $10,000 to upgrade roads in the Township. After my dad accepted, he was told that he needed to go to Quebec City to pick up the cheque. So I drove Dad down to Quebec City. When he came out of his meeting, I asked him "Well, did you get the $10,000?" "No," he responded, "it was for $11,500." Dad explained to me that the amount was adjusted to include support for the Union Nationale party. Dad also told me about the party's close relationship with the Roman Catholic Church and how it quietly reassigned priests who engaged in "double collection" of school taxes – first collecting in cash, then later sending a bill in the mail requesting payment again. (Robert Burns)

Heward Grafftey was a seven-term MP for the Brome-Missisquoi (Quebec) federal riding (who died in 2010 at age 81). He was first elected in 1958 in the heyday of one of the country's last political machines, Maurice Duplessis's Union Nationale. In a 2007 interview with Holly Doan, publisher of *Blacklock's Reporter*, Grafftey recalled those years. Following are excerpts from a transcription of his remarks:

> I was at a hockey game in 1958. Premier Duplessis invited me to come to his box at the old Montreal Forum. He waited for the siren to end the second period, and turned to me and said he knew a Union Nationale organizer who wanted a federal judgeship very, very badly. He looked at me and said, "Look, I'm the premier of Québec and Mr. Diefenbaker is the prime minister of Canada, and I have no right to interfere with his job, but would you tell him I'd like to see this man made a judge?" Of course I did, and he was made a judge. . . There were often kickbacks on road contracts, that sort of thing. Somebody would get a contract, maybe there wasn't open bidding, and it was determined you better give something back to the Party. It wasn't very pleasant, but it was done. It was pervasive. Duplessis was quite a dominating presence. He was The Chief, a tub-thumper, a very charismatic speaker. He was in control of the Party, the whole thing. Politics is kind of an addiction; it gets in your blood, and I guess he just had that.

> In those days the Union Nationale had a tacit agreement with the Church, and the Church was pretty well pro-Duplessis all the time. At election time, The Chief always made sure the parish driveways were paved. Every time they opened a new school, the local bishop would turn up, a big performance, and they'd put a crucifix in every classroom. I suppose some people thought it was sinister, but it really wasn't. Rural, small-town Québec, that's where the majorities were. They liked Duplessis, and they liked what he did, and they supported him. Here in Montréal it wasn't quite the same, but he got his majorities in small-town Québec. . . . There's a famous story: Duplessis in small-town

Québec making a speech. "Vote for my candidate and we're going to build you a bridge." And somebody shouts from the crowd, "But Mr. Duplessis, we don't have a river." "Well," he said, "I'll give you that too!" (Heward Grafftey, blacklocks.ca)

As a postscript to this chapter, it is noted that John French attended Maurice Duplessis's funeral in Quebec City in September 1959.

> Mr. and Mrs. John W. French, with Mr. Ernest Dumont and Mr. Laurent Dumont, N. P., were in Quebec City to join with the many thousands who mourned the passing of the Provincial Premier, the Honourable Maurice L. Duplessis. (*Sherbrooke Daily Record*, Sep. 15, 1959)

Chapter 8
Retirement Living: A Life of Giving

We make a living by what we get. We make a life by what we give. – Winston Churchill

Time (photo by author); Talent (istockphoto; credit Eti Ammos); Treasure (photo by author)

There is no doubt that John and Dorothy French enjoyed success and prosperity in their working lives. Being single and holding responsible positions, they were able to achieve a good level of financial security. This would have allowed them to live comfortably unto themselves in retirement. However, they were not satisfied to just live on their laurels and their rubles. Instead, they lived a retirement life characterized by giving. This chapter looks at how John and Dorothy unsparingly gave of their time, their talents and their treasure for the benefit of others – a benevolence that greatly enhanced the community's social, cultural and spiritual life.

Early retirement

Like most of my contemporaries, I only knew John and Dorothy French in their retirement years. Exactly when their retirement actually began is unclear but it was probably very soon after their marriage in 1935. In any case, John's occupation was specified as "Retired" on the Craig Street house purchase deed. Some family members share similar sentiments.

> I only knew a "retired" Uncle John, busy looking after others, it seemed. (Alice Wickenden MacEwen)

> I didn't know what Uncle John did for work – as far as I knew, he never worked. (John French Wickenden)

Dearly beloved

Community organizations

An excerpt from John French's obituary summarizes very well the attitudes that characterized his and Dorothy's retirement life:

> He was keenly interested in the welfare of the citizens, not only of Cookshire, but of the whole county, and gave unstintingly of his time, talents and money to help improve conditions in this area. (John W. French obituary)

Although some of their contributions were accomplished as a team, many were the result of John and Dorothy "doing their own thing." We will begin with examples of the latter.

Women's Institute

To the women of Cookshire and the surrounding area, Dorothy French's name was closely associated with the Women's Institute. What, really, was this organization? Was it just another sort of "stitch-and-bitch" club? Definitely not. Or was it only a social gathering that provided women with a brief respite from their responsibilities as wives and mothers? No, neither was it that. Rather, it was a sort of an educational forum, think tank and ideas incubator, all rolled into one. The origin of this Canadian home-grown women's organization is very interesting:

> The Women's Institute is a uniquely Canadian contribution to adult education. Rooted in its humble beginnings in rural Ontario, it now has over nine million members in over 70 countries. The Women's Institute's objectives and organizational structure have proven to be of lasting benefit. The Women's Institute was founded in 1897, in Stony Creek, Ont. by Mrs. Adelaide Hoodless based on the premise that "A nation cannot rise above the level of its homes, [therefore] we women must work and study together to raise our homes to the highest level possible." . . . The Women's Institute grew dramatically . . . By 1908 the [organization] had grown to 24 institutes and 4500 members. The first W. I. branches in Quebec were formed in 1911. (ufv.ca)

Its guiding principles are reflected in a "collect" (a prayer) that was repeated at all

---

The Collect

Keep us O Lord from pettiness; let us be large in thought, in word and deed.

Let us be done with fault finding and leave off self seeking.

May we put away all pretence and meet each other face to face, without self pity and without prejudice.

May we never be hasty in judgment and always generous.

Let us take time for all things; make us grow calm, serene, gentle.

Teach us to put into action our better impulses straight forward and unafraid.

Grant that we may realize that it is the little things that create differences; that in the big things of life we are one.

And may we strive to touch and know the great human heart common to us all, and O Lord God let us not forget to be kind.

W. I. Women's Creed by Mary Stewart (peiwi.ca)

meetings – a prayer that coincidently seemed to express so many of Dorothy's own personal ideals.

Dorothy dedicated significant amounts of her time and talent to the Cookshire branch of the W. I., variously serving on the executive, organizing activities and acting as meeting hostess. But she will perhaps be most remembered for her words – both her inspiring literary recitations and her own reflections on topics of the day. Over four decades, her many contributions were noted in the *Record*, a few of which are reproduced here:

> Our organization is dedicated to "Home and Country." We have our contacts, which are indeed precious; and in this non-sectarian non-partisan atmosphere, we try to live up to the high ideals we pray for in the "Club Women's Creed." We miss the absent ones, and we rejoice when they are able to join us again. We share the anxiety and pride of those who have sons and daughters in the services. We sympathize with those who have been bereaved . . .

> In closing, may I leave you the message of Mrs. Harvey Dunham, President of the F. W. I. C., which some of you may have already read: "Nutrition holds with war work, the centre of the stage in our programmes, yet let us ever be conscious of the fact that our future citizens have a mental and moral code to their nature as well as a physical, and all are equally important. This is my 1943 message – Look well to the work that lies nearest, recognize and accept its basic importance – the development of our future citizens, the creating and maintaining of the highest form of morals – and after this 'Whatsoever thy hand findeth to do, do it with all thy might.' Thus will 1943 prove a happy year and bring that best of all gifts, the consciousness of work well done." (*Sherbrooke Daily Record*, Mar. 23, 1943)

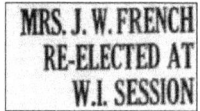

Members and visitors listened with interest to an address by Mrs. John French on "New Canadians in Quebec," which was the special feature of the June meeting of the Cookshire Women's Institute under the convenorship of the citizenship department. Developing the theme that all of us who are not Indian [First Nation] are, in a sense, new Canadians, the speaker dealt in more detail with the two largest ethnic groups, the French-speaking and the English-speaking. In an historical resume, evidently the result of much research, she spoke of the common origin in the Caucasian race. They still retain in some aspects of language and appearance, distinctive marks of this origin.

After many centuries, during which many waves of immigration flowed over Europe, the kingdom of the Franks emerged in what is now France and the kingdoms of the Anglo-Saxons in Britain. After a chequered history, these two ethnic groups met again in New France. In a vivid outline, Mrs. French followed their paths by the way of the early explorers, the traders, the settlers, and the conflicts to their place in the Province of Quebec.

Then she turned to the present "New Canadians," the immigrants of recent years, and the important part they are playing in the development of the country. Among the many interesting facts mentioned were the successful assimilation of a selected group of West Indian girls and the expected arrival of 262 Spaniards. At a recent ceremony in Sherbrooke, persons of 17 different nationalities received citizenship papers. It is planned to have Mrs. French's valuable paper put into permanent form. (*Sherbrooke Daily Record*, June 18, 1957)

On Monday afternoon, February 24th, about forty friends called on Mrs. H. A. Chaddock to congratulate her on the occasion of her 82nd birthday. A small gift was presented by her friends. Mrs. John French made the presentation with an original poem which expressed the high esteem of the community for this worthy citizen. (*Sherbrooke Daily Record*, Mar. 4, 1941)

A special feature of the Women's Institute's meeting was the welcoming and entertaining of the High School teachers. . . At the tea hours, Mrs. J. W. French welcomed the teachers with a few witty remarks and recited a lovely poem. (*Sherbrooke Daily Record,* Sep. 16, 1960)

The ladies of the Women's Institute were privileged to hear the Rev. J. A. Filshie speak on citizenship at the monthly meeting, held June 2 at the home of Mr. and Mrs. John W. French (*Sherbrooke Daily Record*, June 14, 1967)

The work of the Women's Institute, under Dorothy's creative guidance, had impacts on other community organizations. One example is the Compton County Historical and Museum Society. In an address at its House and Garden Tour in 2005, vice-president Richard Faubert paid tribute to the Compton County Women's Institutes for the founding of the Historical and Museum Society. Dorothy played a very active role in this effort.

Richard [Faubert] gives credit to the foresight and diligent hard work of members of the Compton County Women's Institutes, that this Historical Society exists today. The Compton County W. I. was formed in 1912 with the first meeting held in the Trinity United (Methodist) Church in Cookshire. At one time, there were nine W. I. branches in Compton County, and by 1945, over 200 members. (*Sherbrooke Daily Record*, Aug. 17, 2005)

The Eaton Corner museum has, among its collection of historical artifacts, a number of Dorothy's family heirlooms including period costumes and accessories donated by John and Dorothy:

- Two gowns, long white cotton, that belonged to Dorothy's aunt, Miss Mary McLeod, 1875

- Collection of nightgowns, pinafores and baby bonnet belonging to Mary MacLeod, 1875
- Watch chain and compass owned by Dorothy's father, John F. MacLeod in 1870 (Sharon Moore, Eaton Corner Museum)

A Craig Street neighbour, whose grandmother was also a very active member of the Women's Institute, remembers meetings in their home.

> I imagine that with Dorothy's involvement with the Women's Institute, she would have come to "The Evergreens" for W. I. meetings hosted there by [my grandmother] Estelle Frasier. We young kids would have had no interaction with any of the attendees. (Frasier Bellam)

Compton County Agricultural Society

Cookshire Fair Ladies Dept. floral displays, ca. 1960; Cookshire Fair handicraft exhibits, 1989 (both photos by author)

Both John and Dorothy French were strong supporters of the annual Cookshire Fair sponsored by the Compton County Agricultural Society. A search of the Society's records by Neil Burns, a current Fair organizer, revealed the extent of their participation:

Cookshire Fair Ladies Dept. historical display, ca. 1960 (photo by author)

> John was a director of the Fair in the 1940s and 1950s and an honorary director in the 1960s. He also served on the Reception Committee in 1944. Dorothy was an important member of the Ladies Committee, which oversaw the exhibits of handicrafts, cooking, flowers, fruits, vegetables and maple products as well as the various historical displays

upstairs in the Main Building. She served on the Committee in the 1930s, 1940s and 1950s, becoming an honorary member in 1965. (Neil Burns)

Church and charitable causes

Remember this: Whoever sows sparingly will also reap sparingly, and whoever sows generously will also reap generously. Each of you should give what you have decided in your heart to give, not reluctantly or under compulsion, for God loves a cheerful giver. (Bible, 2 Corinthians 9:6-7, New International Version)

St. Peter's Church, Cookshire (photo by author)

Trinity United Church, Cookshire (Conseil du patrmoine religieux du Québec)

It is quite obvious that John and Dorothy lived by the above biblical precept. The local churches – St. Peter's Anglican and Trinity United – both benefitted from John and Dorothy's active participation and generous support, as noted by a pair of fellow parishioners:

> They were faithful church-goers and they lived the life all week. You watched the way they spent their money – it was a learning experience. I don't know if the United Church would have survived without them. (Dorothy Ross)

> My folks often mentioned their names, especially regarding their donations to the Church, including a new furnace after the war. (Charles W. K. Fraser)

As she did in Women's Institute meetings, Dorothy favoured St. Peter's Guild meetings with her recitations and her hospitality:

Retirement Living: a Life of Giving

> The Ladies' Guild of St. Peter's Church was entertained at the residence of Mrs. John W. French. (*Sherbrooke Daily Record*, Oct. 20, 1941)

> St Peter's W. A.: Mrs. John French gave three splendid recitations. (*Sherbrooke Daily Record*, May 3, 1944)

> Mrs. John French entertained the Ladies' Guild of St. Peter's. (*Sherbrooke Daily Record*, Mar. 7, 1947)

For his part, John served in various roles at St. Peter's in addition to making important donations. Some examples follow.

> John W. French was named to the Select Vestry at St Peter's. (*Sherbrooke Daily Record*, Feb. 4, 1961)

> Appointed as Synod Delegates were J. R. French, W. Hamilton, H. C. Barter and J. W. French. (*Sherbrooke Daily Record*, Feb. 19, 1962)

> J. W. French was put in charge of the Osgood Memorial at St Peter's. (*Sherbrooke Daily Record*, Feb. 7, 1963)

> John French has made a donation of an oil furnace to St Peter's Church. (*Sherbrooke Daily Record*, Mar. 7, 1967)

John and Dorothy were generous supporters of the Sherbrooke Hospital. In 1969, John was made a Governor of the hospital.

> J. W. French donated $25. to Sherbrooke Hospital Campaign. (*La Tribune*, Mar. 28, 1953, translated by author)

> J. W. French was made a governor of the Sherbrooke Hospital. (*Sherbrooke Daily Record*, Nov. 6, 1969)

Former Anglican Church, now Community Church, Lawrence Colony, Que. (photo by author)

In the mid-1930s, John was a member of the Eastern Townships Colonization Society that provided support for the new families being settled in Lawrence Colony near Island Brook. Among the projects with which he was involved was the building of a church in the fledgling community.

John's work with the Cookshire Cemetery Association, of which he was president for several years, will be covered in detail in Chapter 13.

Dearly beloved

On April 26, 1936, Sherbrooke's *La Tribune* newspaper reported that John was called for jury duty in the murder trial of Kenneth Brown. However, he was excused from serving because he declared that his mind had already been made up concerning the case.

Support in time of need

John's and Dorothy's deeds of giving were not limited to the organizations described above. No, their unheralded generosity extended far beyond. Following are a few examples of the ways in which they humbly and quietly assisted families and individuals:

> They arranged help for any poor family. Whenever I had anything to do with them, they always made me feel very comfortable even though they had a higher standard of living than we did. (Dorothy Ross)

> [My sister] Martha told me that Uncle John believed that TV was a wonderful companion to home life, so he secretly bought and sent them to those without, who would benefit from having one. (Alice Wickenden MacEwen)

> Uncle John once bought a telephone for a friend from whom he never heard. This would make it easy for his friend to contact him. After a few weeks of no calls, we drove out there and found that the man didn't know how to use the phone! It was one rainy day when I worked on the farm and we didn't work. That was Uncle John doing his thing, looking after others. (John French Wickenden)

It wasn't only to material needs that John and Dorothy responded. They were there in times of sickness and at times of death:

> The many friends of Miss Annie E. McDonald will be interested to know that she is now at the Hôpital de Sacrement in Sherbrooke. Miss McDonald suffered a setback on January 20, and although she is gaining slowly, she is still bedridden. On Monday, Mr. T. C. French conveyed her by ambulance from Scotstown to Sherbrooke and she was accompanied by Mr. John French. (*Sherbrooke Daily Record*, Mar. 19, 1951)

> Mrs. McHardy has gone to Boston, Mass., where she has entered the Lahey clinic for treatment. She was accompanied by Mrs. John French. (*Sherbrooke Daily Record*, May 5, 1941)

> On different occasions, bedridden Lilla Fraser noted in her diary that John had come for a visit. One example: March 27, 1947: John French visit. (Lilla J. Fraser diary)

> When my grandmother Estelle Frasier was in the hospital in Sherbrooke and passed away there, the hospital phoned John, and asked him to

come over to our house to tell Mom, who was working in our garden. (Frasier Bellam)

John French was a bearer at Jed Fraser's funeral. (*Sherbrooke Daily Record*, May 5, 1952) *(Author's note: He was a bearer at many other funerals in Cookshire and elsewhere.)*

Generosity to family

Amidst their busyness looking after folks in the community, their own family was not forgotten, as demonstrated by the latter's testimonies.

> During and immediately after World War II, our family were excited around Christmas time when parcels would arrive from Canada – Uncle Horace and family in Wetaskiwin, Alberta, Aunt Ellen, as well as Uncle John and Aunt Dorothy in Cookshire and Aunt Nellie Bailey too. (Roger Lancey)

> Christmas gifts from them were always books, carefully chosen by Dorothy, I am sure. (Martha Wickenden MacKellar)

> My occasional work for them consisted of picking a bouquet or running an errand to another shed that led to another shed. I remember remuneration sometimes – a dime or a nickel, Big Money then! (Alice Wickenden MacEwen)

> On leaving Cookshire, John gave me $30 "for your train fare," he said – very generous of him, going well beyond the cost of the fare at that time! He was not only kind, generous and hospitable, but even at age 82, still interested in what everyone was doing . . . (Roger Lancey)

My own family also benefited from the Frenches' generosity, as illustrated by the following examples:

> My fondest memory was John French gifting me a brand new 3-speed bike on April 27, 1962! My old one-speed CCM model was always breaking down. It was so unexpected! After that, it was hard to turn down his calls for help – often on a moment's notice. (Steve Fraser)

> John French was a good man and the Fraser family was well respected in the town. So of course John wanted to help them out. They were a large family. He paid for the oldest children to go to college, with the intention that the older ones would in turn help the younger ones. I learned this from Dorothy at [St. Peter's] Church. For a short while – one winter I guess it was – we had small prayer groups of five or six people where we confided in each other. (Dorothy Ross)

Recognitions and memorials

John and Dorothy French were not the kind of persons who craved attention and accolades for their good deeds. Nonetheless, they did receive a number of well-deserved recognitions, both in their later years of life and after they had passed into eternal rest. Some that were reported in the *Record* are presented below:

The May meeting of the Women's Institute was held at the home of Mrs. D. L. Pope, when the special feature of the meeting was the presentation of a Life Membership to Mrs. J. W. French by Mrs. R. B. Learned, County President. (*Sherbrooke Daily Record*, May 21, 1960)

Women's Institute Life Member medal (pinterest.ca)

The Compton County Women's Institute has been awarding bursaries for 20 years to students leaving high school for further studies . . . A special third bursary was decided on for this year in honour of Dorothy and John French, late of Cookshire. Dorothy was a devoted member of the Cookshire Women's Institute and both she and John were noted for their public spirit and good works. (*Sherbrooke Daily Record*, Oct. 18, 1971)

The altar rails, which formerly were used in the Chapel of the Venerable Bede of Bishop's University, have been restored and placed in St. Peter's Church in Cookshire, in memory of the late John W. French, and will be rededicated by the Rev. J. D. F. Anido, of Bishop's University on Dec. 1st, at the 11 am service. (*Sherbrooke Daily Record*, Nov. 20, 1974)

Cookshire United Church annual meeting: It was stated that $500.00 had been received for the 1971 budget from the estate of the late Mrs. John W. French (Sherbrooke Daily Record, Feb. 8, 1971)

Mr. Malcolm Fraser presented the Church wardens' financial statement, which showed a credit balance after all expenses had been paid. It was decided to transfer part of the John W. French legacy to the endowments. (*Sherbrooke Daily Record*, Feb. 4, 1972)

A meeting of the Lewis Cemeteries Association was held Friday evening, July 21, in the Presbyterian church, Scotstown. . . The two trust funds were reported on by the secretary. The John W. French fund, and the Savings & Investment fund received favourable comment as there will be over $2000. available for distribution to cemeteries in the area. (*Sherbrooke Daily Record*, Aug. 2, 1972)

St. Peters Church Cookshire altar rail and altar (photos by author)

Dearly beloved

Chapter 9
Salute to Siblings

To the outside world we all grow old. But not to brothers and sisters. We know each other as we always were. We know each other's hearts. We share private family jokes. We remember family feuds and secrets, family griefs and joys. We live outside the touch of time. – Clara Ortega, Spanish author

Back Row - Ronnie Buckle, Aunt Annie, Uncle John, Margaret Buckle, Uncle Malcolm
Front Row: Aunt Lottie, Aunt Dorothy, Uncle Horace
August 1966

French family gathering during Horace and Annie visit in 1966 (courtesy of Ken Watson)

John French and siblings, 1893. Clockwise from top: Charles, Martha, Horace, Lottie, John (courtesy of Ken Watson)

Although John and Dorothy had no children of their own, they were blessed with a large family. This chapter focuses on the folks who made up that family – siblings, nieces, nephews, grandnieces and grandnephews. Because family was such an important part of their lives, we have dedicated an entire chapter to it. We preface this salute to siblings and their families with a simple multiple-choice math question:

How many siblings in total did John and Dorothy have?
- 7
- 8.5
- 10
- All of the above
- None of the above

Horace, Charlie and John, Cookshire, 1948
(courtesy of Leslie Buckle)

And . . . the correct answer is . . . (*read backwards*) "evoba eht fo lla."

Yes indeed – all of the above! Before you think I have lost my (mathematical) mind, I will explain. John and Dorothy, you see, had seven full siblings and three half-siblings. So, depending on how you count them, you could arrive at any of the three different totals. However, were John and Dorothy still with us in the flesh, they would most certainly insist they had ten siblings. In their mind, there was no distinction between full siblings and half siblings – they loved them all equally.

Margaret Mackenzie, Catherine Jean Wickenden, Martha Louise Wickenden, Don French, Mary Mackenzie, Roddy French, Rhona Mackenzie & Ruth Mackenzie

Eight French, Wickenden and Mackenzie cousins
(courtesy of Ken Watson)

Each of the siblings has a life story to tell, whether it be told from the recollections of family and friends or from newspaper reports, diary entries and family archives. Below, in order of their birthdates, we present John and Dorothy's ten siblings.

Persis Harriet French ("Pertie"), 1875-1938

Pertie was the first-born of the three children of Charles Ward Bailey French and his first wife, Maria A. Bailey. (Her father would later have seven additional children with his second wife, Catherine "Kate" McIver.)

Pertie was disabled her entire life and required continuous care, which was provided by her mother, then by her aunts and her stepmother, and finally by her sister Ellen. From time to time, her brother John would drive her different places to visit other family members. Occasionally, Cookshire friends would help out with her care. Although I was not able to learn the exact nature of her infirmities, one of her grandnieces shared information that provides some clues:

Charles W. B. French family, 1896 (*History of Compton County*)

With respect to her illness, my mother [Jocelyn Wickenden Watson] used to say that Aunt Pertie was pretty much bedridden, and had the stature of a child. I had her crutches once upon a time, and played with them endlessly as a 7- and 8-year-old child. They fit me back then – but by the time I was 10, they were too short for me – which gives some indication of Pertie's height. My mother also described Aunt Pertie as "gentle," and said that she could only speak a few words. My mother, in fact, only remembered Aunt Pertie ever saying "My, my." My mother – as a little girl – would sit on Aunt Pertie's bed, and tell her all sorts of stories about whatever was of interest to her, and Aunt Pertie would smile, shake her head, and say in a soft, gentle voice, "My, my." My mother said Aunt Pertie made her feel very special. She loved Aunt Pertie dearly. (Mary Watson)

Social notes in the local newspapers kept the townsfolk apprised of Pertie's state of health as well as her comings and goings:

The Misses Pertie and Ellen French, of Scotstown, were in town [Cookshire] over Sunday. (*Sherbrooke Examiner*, Aug. 13, 1902)

Mrs. Hollis Osgood and Miss Persis French are far from being as well as their friends would wish. (*Sherbrooke Daily Record*, Nov. 16, 1922)

Mr. J. French and sisters, Ellen, Persis and Annie and his mother, Mrs. C. W. B. French, were in town [Gould] on Sunday. (*Sherbrooke Daily Record*, Nov. 17, 1923)

Misses Ellen and Persis French, who have been spending the winter months with Mrs. Charles W. B. French and Mr. John W. French, are contemplating returning to their home on Craig Street shortly, which is now occupied by Mr. and Mrs. H. Ashley Sheltus. (*Sherbrooke Daily Record*, Mar. 6, 1926)

Pertie French scrapbook front cover with inscription (courtesy of Mary Watson)

Miss Pertie French was remembered on Sunday, November 22nd, with a birthday card shower from a host of friends. Miss French's condition shows a very slight improvement and all hope that she will continue to gain. (*Sherbrooke Daily Record*, Nov. 27, 1931)

Mrs. H. H. Pope is helping to care for Miss Persis French for a short time. (*Sherbrooke Daily Record*, July 16, 1932)

Mrs. Frank Kingsley attended the funeral of Miss Persis French, at Cookshire (*Sherbrooke Daily Record*, May 19, 1938)

Pertie French scrapbook inside page collage (courtesy of Mary Watson)

Grandniece Mary recently re-discovered her Great-aunt Pertie's scrapbook, whose pages were filled with colourful Christmas cards, calling cards and clippings of inspirational poems. The book must have been a source of joy for Pertie amidst her affliction.

Niece Martha had a special connection to her Aunt Pertie:

Aunt Pertie (Persis) was my godmother. I was christened in Cookshire at St. Peter's Church on Oct. 19, 1930. Aunt Ellen stood proxy for Pertie, who was an invalid – always bedridden as I recall. I have no idea what she suffered from. Long-suffering Ellen carried that burden. (Martha Wickenden MacKellar)

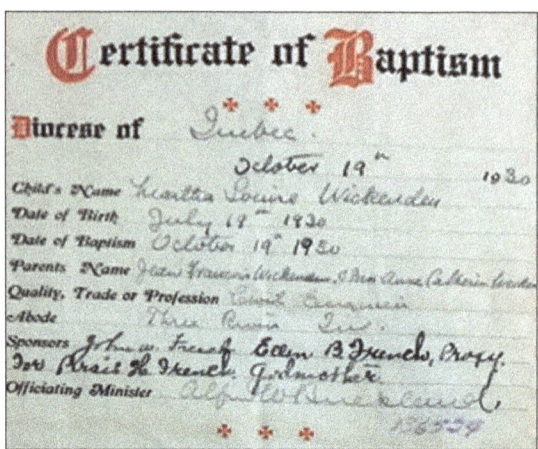

Martha Wickenden MacKellar Certificate of Baptism (courtesy of Martha Wickenden MacKellar)

Cookshire gathering, ca. 1930. Back, L-R: Ellen, Mrs. Rooney, Pertie, Kate; front, L-R: Margaret Darker, Rod French, Dr. Robert Rooney, Horace, Charlie (courtesy of Leslie Buckle)

Ellen Bailey French, 1878-1964

As mentioned above, Ellen was, for many years, the primary care-giver for her older sister, Pertie. However, prior to that she spent several years in Montreal. Ellen's obituary provides the details:

> Ellen was born in Scotstown, the second child of Charles W. B. French and Maria A. Bailey. Following her father's death in 1905, she came to

live in Cookshire, where she graduated from the Academy and then attended Normal School in Montreal. After teaching for a few years, she returned to Cookshire to live with her aunts, the Misses Abbie and Ann Bailey and her invalid sister, Pertie. After their deaths, she remained in Cookshire. She was a faithful member of St. Peter's Church, was active in the Guild and a supporter of all worthy causes. (*Sherbrooke Daily Record*, July 15, 1964)

Drawing by Ellen French, 1890 (courtesy of Mary Watson)

Postcard of "Court of the Universe," San Francisco World's Fair, 1915 (ebay.com)

Dearly beloved

From sheets hidden tucked inside her sister Pertie's scrapbook, it was discovered by her grandniece Mary Watson that Ellen was a budding artist at the age of 12.

According to her grandnephew Roger, Ellen took a major trip in 1915.

> Ellen went with William and Laura Bailey (brother and sister, and her uncle and aunt), on a journey through western Canada, visiting [her brother] Horace in Wetaskiwin, Alberta, and then on to the San Francisco Fair in 1915. (Roger Lancey)

Ellen's nieces and nephews remember her hospitality when they came to Cookshire to spend time with the French family:

> One summer when I spent happy time with Marina [Fraser] et al, I stayed with Aunt Ellen for a week. It was a long week. She told me one evening, when I went out and danced about on her lawn for release from the house, "Oh, Alice, you are just like Annie." Another evening, she allowed, bitterly, "I was the work horse of the family." I was unaware of a huge part of her life of work. I did not know she had been a teacher and taught for a year in Trois-Rivières. But I did know that she was a Bailey! We all regret the questions we didn't ask. I was more concerned that evening with the half-piece of liver on my plate at supper. I was not a liver lover but I ate it. (Alice Wickenden MacEwen)

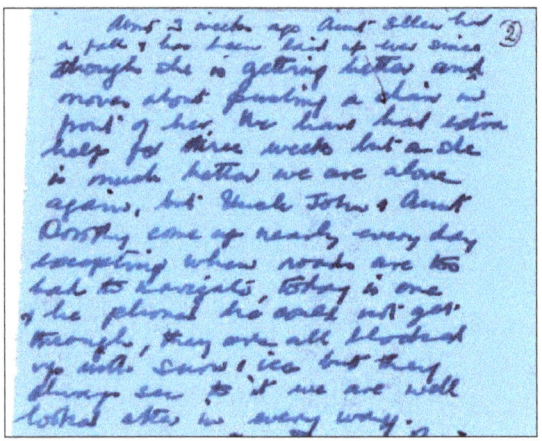

Extract of letter from Bea French to grandson Roger, Feb. 3, 1963 (courtesy of Roger Lancey)

> Aunt Ellen lived just up the road from your [Fraser] farm. She was a very sweet lady. I remember once when stooking grain at your farm on a very hot day, she gave me a quart of water to drink. Even though visits there as a kid were primarily with her sisters and we were not the main event, we were always well-considered. (John French Wickenden)

> My grandmother [Beatrice French] spent several long visits [from the UK to Cookshire] – perhaps two or three years at a time – staying with Ellen between 1947 and 1963. (Roger Lancey)

Other family visits to Ellen's home were noted in the *Record*:

> Master Donald and Miss Enid French, of Montreal, were guests, last week, of Mrs. C. W. B. French and the Misses Ellen and Pertie French. (*Sherbrooke Daily Record*, Aug. 26, 1930)

Mrs. Herbert French visits Ellen French. (*Sherbrooke Daily Record*, June 26, 1956)

Ellen's caregiving extended beyond the walls of her Craig Street home as indicated by visits to my own invalid grandmother:

- June 9, 1945: Ellen French visit all day.
- Oct. 19, 1949: PM visits from Ellen French and Mrs. [John] French (Lilla J. Fraser diary)

Particularly in her later years, Ellen was the beneficiary of her brother John and sister-in-law Dorothy's loving care. Their care and concern for her is referenced in a letter shared by one of her grandnephews:

> About three weeks ago, Aunt Ellen had a fall & has been laid up ever since though she is getting better and moves about pushing a chair in front of her. We have had extra help for three weeks but now she is much better; we are alone again, but Uncle John & Aunt Dorothy came up nearly every day excepting when roads are too bad to navigate, today is one & he phoned he could not get through, they are all blocked up with snow and ice but they always see to it we are well looked after in every way. (Roger Lancey letter from grandmother Bea French, Feb. 3, 1963)
>
> (Author's note: Cookshire weather, according to my mom's diary: Jan. 27: "10 below, cold, windy, snow all day, about 12 inches fell." Jan. 28: "Windy, snow plow went by twice, some roads blocked, no school." Feb. 2: "Snowing most of day, 6 inches fell.")

Personally, I knew Ellen for only the final ten or so years of her life. But during that time I saw her almost daily because I delivered milk and cream on my way to school and brought her mail on the way home. I remember her as a very kind and loving soul. On Christmas mornings I would pay her a special "Merry Christmas" visit on my way to church at St. Peter's.

My younger cousin Frasier, a close neighbour of Ellen, also remembers her:

> Ellen French lived right across the street from [my family's home] "The Evergreens." My only memory is that she was a "nice little old lady." (Frasier Bellam)

Herbert Arthur French, 1880-1916

Herbert was the third child of Charles Ward Bailey French and Maria A. Bailey. Like his two older

Herbert French (courtesy of Judy Moorey)

siblings, he was born at the Scotstown Hotel operated by his parents.

As an adult, Herbert lived in Montreal and worked as a trainman for the Grand Trunk Railway. Tragically, he was killed in a railway accident at the young age of 36. Little detail is known about the circumstances of the tragedy apart from two brief mentions in local newspapers.

> Mr. Herbert A. French of Montreal, formerly of Scotstown and son of the late C. W. B. French of that town, was accidentally killed at Acton vale, Que. on September 12th. He had been in the employ of the Grand Trunk Railway as trainmen for several years between Island Pond [Vermont] and Montreal. The accident occurred last Wednesday while on duty at Acton vale. (*Sherbrooke Daily Record*, Sep. 19, 1916)

FATAL ACCIDENT AT ACTONVALE

CIRCUMSTANCES OF DEATH OF HERBERT FRENCH, SON OF LATE C.W.B. FRENCH, FORMERLY OF SCOTS-TOWN.

Mr. Herbert A. French of Montreal, formerly of Scotstown and son of the late C. W. B. French of that town was accidently killed at Actonvale, Que., September 13th. He had been in the employ of the Grand Trunk Railway as trainman for several years between Island Pond and Montreal. The accident occurred last Wednesday evening while on duty at Actonvale.

His remains were brought to Cookshire for burial. The deceased leaves to mourn his loss a wife and three small children as well as a large number of relatives and friends.

Herbert French accident death notice (*Sherbrooke Daily Record*, Sep. 19, 1916)

Under the headline SAINT-HYACINTHE DISTRICT INQUESTS, the French-language newspaper *Courier St-Hyacinthe* reported on January 6, 1917 that a coroner's inquest had been held "on the body of Herbert-Arthur French, brakeman, who was killed in a collision, at Acton-Vale." Efforts to obtain additional details have been without success. The epitaph on Herbert's gravestone expectantly states "Sometime we'll understand."

Herbert French gravestone epitaph, Cookshire Cemetery (courtesy of Roger Lancey)

Beatrice and family: Ruth, Eunice, Garth, Muriel (below right) and picture of father Herbert French (courtesy of Judy Moorey)

Herbert was married to Sarah Beatrice "Bea" French from Worcestershire in the UK and they had four children.

After World War I, Bea decided to return to her parents in the UK with her children. Their departure, as well as her family news and return visits were reported in the *Record*'s social notes. Beatrice's grandson, Roger Lancey, remarked that "she loved Cookshire, and I know the folk there loved her being with them."

> Mrs. Herbert French who has been residing here [Cookshire] for about two years, intends sailing this month for England to visit her parents and other relatives and she will be accompanied by her four children, the Misses Ruth, Lois and Muriel French and Master Garth French. (*Sherbrooke Daily Record*, June 2, 1919)

> The sad news has been received from England, of the death of Garth French, aged sixteen years, only son of Mrs. Herbert French and the late Mr. French, formerly of this place. The sympathy of the community is extended to the bereaved relatives. (*Sherbrooke Daily Record*, June 28, 1932)

> Mrs. Herbert French, of Worcester, England, is spending an indefinite time with Miss Ellen French. (*Sherbrooke Daily Record*, June 26, 1956)

> Miss Lucy Hodge entertained the Guild of St. Peter's Church on Sept. 9. Mrs. A. W. Standish presided and welcomed Mrs. Herbert French of London, England. (*Sherbrooke Daily Record*, Sep. 22, 1964)

Charles Daniel French, 1884-1954

Charles (or "C. D." as he was commonly known to people outside the family) was the first-born of Charles Ward Bailey French's "second" family (i.e., from his marriage to Catherine "Kate" McIver). Charles's very interesting and productive life is perhaps best summarized in the biography published on the Quebec National Assembly website:

Charles Daniel French (ancestry.com)

> Born in Scotstown on January 26, 1884, son of Charles French, hotelkeeper, and Kate MacIver. Educated in Scotstown. Farmer in Cookshire. President of Kennedy Construction Co. Ltd. of Montreal from 1919 to 1946. Member of the Canadian Club of Montreal. Defeated Union Nationale candidate for Compton in 1939. Elected Union Nationale MLA for the same riding in

a July 3, 1946 by-election. Re-elected in 1948 and 1952. Minister of Mines in the Duplessis cabinet from December 15, 1948 to May 3, 1954. Died in office in Westmount on May 3, 1954 at the age of 70 years and 3 months. Interred in the Cookshire Cemetery on May 7, 1954. Was married in the Scotstown Presbyterian Church on January 1, 1914, to Emily Christina Macauley, daughter of Malcolm B. Macauley, entrepreneur and Emma M. Bailey. (assnat.qc.ca)

Cromwell residence, the future C. D. French home, Cookshire, ca. 1930 (courtesy of Ken Watson)

Cromwell House, former C. D. French home, Cookshire, 2020 (duproprio.com)

A fascinating incident occurred during a road-building project while Charles was president of Kennedy Construction:

> In August, 1942, workers engaged by the Kennedy Construction company made a ghastly discovery. While digging a passenger tunnel under the city approach to the Victoria Bridge, they unearthed twelve "coffins of rotting pine wood, blackened by time," in "a long trench like grave at the foot of Bridge Street." The Irish community sought permission from the CNR and Anglican leadership to re-bury the deceased at the site of the monument. Permission was granted, and the bones were reinterred close to the Irish Stone, in plain grey caskets, during an All Saints Day ceremony on November 1, 1942. The discovery put to rest any denial that the site was, in fact, a cemetery. (montrealirishmonument.com)

In Cookshire, "C. D." had acquired the Cromwell property where he established a prize-winning herd of purebred Hereford cattle under the management of chief herdsman Pete Macdonald.

C. D. French grand champion Hereford bull, Sherbrooke Fair (banq.qc.ca)

His nephews and nieces, who knew him simply as "Uncle Charlie," share a variety of memories:

> When Mother taught in Montreal she lived with Aunt Emily and Uncle Charlie. She spoke of evenings when she sat near him on a foot stool and he would say, "There's nothing like my own kith and kin." Annie, teaching in St. Urbain, fascinated with the side locks on the little boys she taught, found it cold. Charlie bought her a fur coat. He was a caring man. I am sure Lottie was on the receiving end of many carefully chosen gifts too. (Alice Wickenden MacEwen)
>
> In the summers of 1949 and 1950, I worked on Uncle Charlie's farm during the month of August. I stayed at the farm. My dad had taught me

how to drive at an early age, because we used to go hunting together. So I got to drive the tractor baling grain, then stooking, then loading onto the wagons. I learned what hard work farming was. It was tough working with men but it was an experience that shaped my life. (John French Wickenden)

On rainy days, a few times I went with Uncle Charlie, who was a Member of Parliament, to visit somebody. I would drive! One day, we were on a newly paved road, which suddenly became gravel about 500 yards down the road and then was pavement again. When I asked why, his reply was, "He's a Liberal." That was how it was. (John French Wickenden)

Mother adored him. Uncle Charlie slurped his soup. We were in trouble if **we** did so. But we were admonished to give NO INDICATION AT ALL that slurping was out of the ordinary when he was there at lunch time, between trains from Montreal to Quebec. And we didn't. Every Christmas he gave Mother a FIVE pound box of Leonie Chocolates. We might get one each. The box disappeared after that. Years later I learned that she kept it in her bedroom cupboard. Solace of a sort when days needed comfort food! (Alice Wickenden MacEwen)

One time when I was 14 years old, visiting with Uncle Charlie and Aunt Emily [in Montreal], he asked me if I liked hockey. "Yes" I replied. "Would I like to go to a game?" he asked. "But you can't get tickets" I said. "Well," he said, "I know a man who knows a man . . ." End of conversation; we went to the Forum, and I saw my beloved team for the first time ever – Richard, Mosdell, Lach, Blake, Harvey, Bouchard, Reardon, Durnan . . . (John French Wickenden)

Another time we went to Lennoxville because he wanted to change his Cadillac for a new one. We parked in front of the dealer; I waited for five minutes or so. When he returned, asking him if he had bought a new car, his reply, "He didn't have time to talk to me." I learned something about sales that day! But he was a good guy, and would wake me every morning at the farm. "Johnny Bateese, Johnny Bateese" he would say. It was 6 AM and we started at 7. Every evening it was Bull's Head ginger ale and grape juice. (John French Wickenden)

Uncle Charlie and Aunt Emily's visits to his mother and John in Cookshire were regularly reported in the *Record*:

Mr.and Mrs. Charles French and their two children, Master Donald and Miss Enid French, were weekend visitors at the home of Mrs. C. W. B. French. (*Sherbrooke Daily Record*, Oct. 11, 1930)

His son, Donald, remembers his father as being "a very giving type of man and was busy as a Member of Parliament." As an MLA and Minster of Mines, C. D. French was greatly appreciated for what he did for the people of Compton County as well as for mining development in the province. Following are some examples of how he helped individuals and businesses:

In 1951 I wrote to C. D. in the spring regarding the possibility of a summer job. He responded right back, telling me "You will have a job . . . down in the Gaspé where you will be a travelling companion for geologist George Mueller." So I took the train to Grand Cascapedia and spent the summer taking geological readings in the mountains and the streams. (Carl Jackson)

I worked the summer of '53 at C. D. French's farm with the Mcdonald crew. They made hard work haying on a hot day enjoyable. (Stanley Parker)

Hon. C. D. French Turns First Sod For New Asbestos Plant And Mill

CD French turns first sod for asbestos plant (*Sherbrooke Daily Record*, June 17, 1952)

In June 1952, C. D. turned the sod for a major new asbestos mining and processing plant. How ironic it is that now, some 70 years later, asbestos mining in Quebec has been completely shut down and that industry has become such a pariah that the town of Asbestos has decided to change its name! In fact, as I am writing this, the new name has just been announced: Val-des-Sources.

Charles Daniel passed away on May 3, 1954. His funeral at St. Peter's Church in Cookshire was a very major event with many dignitaries, including Premier Duplessis and his entire cabinet, in attendance. I was in Grade 4 at the time and recall we were given time off class to watch the sombre proceedings at the neighbouring church.

C. D. French funeral (*Sherbrooke Daily Record*, May 8, 1954)

Malcolm Fraser receiving C. D. French beef judging trophy, 1960 (Fraser family archives)

Following his passing, a pair of awards were instituted in memory of C. D. and in recognition of his lifelong interest in agriculture, especially the raising of quality beef cattle. The C. D. French Bursary was established as an annual monetary gift to a graduating Compton County high school student going on to higher education. I had the honour of receiving this award in 1961. The C. D. French trophy was awarded annually to the young farmer who placed first in 4-H beef judging competitions. My late brother, Malcolm ("Mac"), won this award in both 1960 and 1961.

Mary Isabella French, 1885-1891

John French had two sisters who died in childhood. Mary Isabella was the first. Unfortunately, we have no information or photograph of little Mary Isabella, who passed away at the age of six years.

Mary Isabella French gravestone, Cookshire Cemetery (courtesy of Leslie Nutbrown)

Martha Maud Maria French, 1887-1901

Martha Maud Maria was the second sibling who died at a very early age. I am told that she was afflicted with Bright's disease and passed away at 14 years of age.

Martha Maud Maria French, 1893 (courtesy of Ken Watson)

Bright's disease is a historical term that is not currently in use. It referred to a group of kidney diseases – in modern medicine, the condition is described as acute or chronic nephritis. The disease was named after Richard Bright, who was the first to describe the symptoms in 1827. (news-medical.net)

In the final months of her very short life, the *Sherbrooke Examiner* updated the community on her deteriorating condition.

We regret that little Martha French is not rapidly improving from her severe illness. Much sympathy is felt for all the family as Martha is a special favourite among all her little playmates who are manifesting their love by their gifts of flowers to their little friend. (*Sherbrooke Examiner*, Aug. 1, 1900)

The friends of Martha French will be sorry to hear she is not improving. (*Sherbrooke Examiner*, Sep. 3, 1900)

Martha's 4-year-old sister, Annie, recalled that very sad time:

I remember Mother [Annie French Wickenden] telling me that when her sister Martha was ill and dying, she would sometimes stand outside the bedroom door and ask "Want a drink of water, Mattie?" (Alice Wickenden MacEwen)

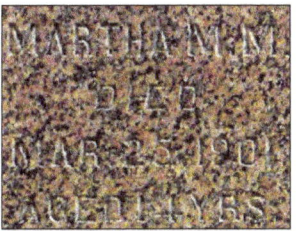

Martha Maud French gravestone, Cookshire Cemetery (courtesy of Leslie Nutbrown)

Eva Mary MacLeod, 1889-1984

Continuing in birthdate sequence, we come to Dorothy's lone sibling, her sister, Eva Mary MacLeod. Born in 1889 – two years before Dorothy – evidence reveals that the two were very close, both age-wise and relationship-wise. For example, they were attendants at each other's weddings and they frequently visited each other's homes in spite of the distance that separated them. Furthermore, as John and Dorothy's mail delivery boy for several years, I can attest to the fact they frequently exchanged letters.

The earliest document we discovered relating to Eva was her registration of birth and baptism in the old Bury Methodist Church.

Eva Mary MacLeod birth (1889) and baptism (1896) record (ancestry.ca)

Eva worked for the Canadian Bank of Commerce, first in Sherbrooke and later in Toronto. The *Record* noted her move and the associated send-off activities:

Miss Eva McLeod, who has been on the staff of the Canadian Bank of Commerce in Sherbrooke, is leaving shortly for Toronto, to take a similar position in the head office in that city. (*Sherbrooke Daily Record*, Mar. 27, 1912)

At the close of the usual meeting, the Y. P. S. C. K., St. Andrew's Church, last evening, a pleasant social hour was spent by the members of the Society and their friends to bid Farewell to Miss Eva MacLeod, who is leaving the city to reside in Toronto. An address was presented to Miss MacLeod from the Christian Endeavour Society, conveying to her their appreciation of the work she has done and expressing regret at losing her from the Society. An address was also presented from the Sabbath School, thanking Miss MacLeod for the valuable services she has rendered in the different departments of the school and wishing her success in her new sphere. The Rev. J. C. Nicholson replied on behalf of Miss MacLeod, thanking those present for the beautiful addresses and kind thoughtfulness. After a short musical programme and the serving of refreshments, the evening terminated with the singing of Auld Lang Syne and God Save the King. (*Sherbrooke Daily Record*, Mar. 26, 1912)

A number of friends of Miss Eva McLeod gathered at the G. T. R. station yesterday to wish her good-bye on the occasion of her departure for Toronto, where she enters upon her duties in the Canadian Bank of Commerce. (*Sherbrooke Daily Record*, Mar. 30, 1912)

Eva was married in 1915 and went to live with her husband in New York City:

A quiet but very pretty wedding was solemnized at the home of Mr. and Mrs. John F. MacLeod, Bury, on Wednesday, September 8, when their daughter, Eva Mary, was united in marriage to Harry Whitcher Shirreffs, of New Yok City, formerly of Sherbrooke. . . After the wedding luncheon, the bridal couple left by motor for Montreal, from whence they will proceed by way of the Lakes and Hudson River to New York, where they will reside. (*Sherbrooke Daily Record*, Sep. 8, 1915)

Although now separated by a significant distance from her family, Eva and Harry frequently returned to the Eastern Townships to visit. Her sister Dorothy reciprocated those visits, as regularly noted in the *Record*:

Mr. Harry Shirreffs, of New York, has joined Mrs. Shirreffs at the home of her parents, Mr. and Mrs. John F. McLeod, to spend his vacation here. (*Sherbrooke Daily Record*, Sep. 4, 1920)

Mrs. Harry Shirreffs, who has been spending several weeks here with her parents, Mr. and Mrs. John F. MacLeod, left on Wednesday last week for her home in New York. Mrs. Shirreffs motored to Quebec for the previous week-end. (*Sherbrooke Daily Record,* Sep. 24, 1924)

Mrs. Harry W. Shirreffs and Miss Dorothy Shirreffs have returned to their home, in New York City, after spending a few weeks with the former's mother, Mrs. J. F. McLeod. (*Sherbrooke Daily Record*, Oct. 20, 1930)

Mr. and Mrs. John W. French spent a few weeks in Bronxville, New York as guests of Mrs. French's sister, Mrs. H. W. Shirreffs, and Mr. Shirreffs. (*Sherbrooke Daily Record*, Oct. 24, 1940)

Eva and Harry had one child, a daughter, Dorothy Elinor MacLeod Shirreffs, whose wedding was attended by her Uncle John and Aunt Dorothy. It is interesting to note that the wedding took place at the same home where John and Dorothy tied the knot 15 years earlier.

Mr. and Mrs. John W. French have returned home from Bronxville, N.Y., where they were the guests of Mr. and Mrs. Harry Shirreffs. On June 24, they attended the wedding of their niece, Miss Dorothy Shirreffs, which took place at the home of her parents. Mr. and Mrs. Kressman will reside in Cleveland, Ohio. (*Sherbrooke Daily Record*, July 12, 1950)

John French, Eva MacLeod Shirreffs and Dorothy French, Bronxville, N.Y., 1955 (courtesy of Kathi Kressman)

Dorothy Elinor MacLeod Shirreffs portrait (ancestry.ca); her gravestone, Lower Brandywine Presbyterian Church Cemetery, Owls Nest, Del. (findagrave.com)

Horace Roderick French, 1890-1974

Never having had the opportunity to meet Horace, I turned to his obituary to learn the details of his very interesting life. Following are extracts from his life story.

Dearly beloved

French's Jewellers, Wetaskiwin, Alta., 1966 (courtesy of Roger Lancey)

Inside Horace French jewellery shop, Wetaskiwin (City of Wetaskiwin archives)

Horace with sister Annie and grandkids Margie and Doug, Wetaskiwin, 1961 (courtesy of Margie French)

John, Dorothy and Horace; Pigeon Lake, Alta., ca. 1950 (courtesy of Margie French)

Horace French was a well-known and respected businessman of this community [Wetaskiwin, Alta.] for over 60 years. . . Up until February of 1973, he spent each and every day in his jewelry store repairing watches, selling items of jewelry, discussing local and national topics of the day or spinning tales about his friends and experiences of an earlier time. He possessed a rare sense of humour and was not above playing a practical joke on any of his friends who were the least bit unwary. . .

"Frenchie" was born in Scotstown, Quebec, March 10, 1890, where he received his education and began his lifetime work in the repair and jewelry trade. On November 8, 1909, Mr. French began work in the jewelry store of C. C. Bailey in Wetaskiwin. . . After serving in the Royal Flying Corps as a pilot in the First World War, "Frenchie" returned and purchased the jewelry store from Mr. Thomas in 1921. "Frenchie" was married to Angie Angus in 1920 and to this union was born two sons, Charles Roderick and Malcolm Angus.

Scotstown postcard, 1906 (courtesy of Evelyn Yvonne Theriault)

He was also a practicing optometrist for many years . . . Sports were a main interest in his life and he played both baseball and hockey on the Wetaskiwin teams in the early days. He was also an ardent hunter and a keen fisherman.

He was quick to perceive what was right with the world, quick to recognize what needed changing, and equally quick to condemn those areas which were wrong and beyond changing. What's more he didn't mince words. (*Sherbrooke Daily Record*, July 8, 1974)

Horace's granddaughter, Donna, retains very fond memories of her Grandpa even though she was a young teenager when he passed away:

He always had time for his four grandchildren. I remember we shared every holiday with them at their home . . . I can still see my Grandpa as he carved the Christmas and Thanksgiving turkeys right at the dining room table! He always had a dime for me to go to the Chinese restaurant, which was next to the jewelry store, to buy a chocolate bar! After buying the bar and going back to the jewelry store, he would always have a story for me about how he knew Little Miss Muffet's father! Grandpa loved his fishing. That was his favorite pastime, and when he wasn't able to fish, he would practice casting his line in their backyard, and reeling it in! I can still see him doing that. (Donna Mikulecky)

Horace and Annie French, Wetaskiwin, Alta., 1966 (courtesy of Roger Lancey)

Horace's nieces and nephews also share memories of their colourful western uncle:

There is a lovely "piece" in the small book *Glimpses of the Past* by Bertha Weston Price, published by the *Sherbrooke Daily Record* in January 1955, describing a banquet given for Charles C. Bailey, younger son of Cyrus A. Bailey, in July 1904, giving him a "send off," as he was "travelling west" to Wetaskiwin to set up a "watchmaking and jewelry shop" there. It was this venture that Uncle Horace joined in 1909, and later continued the business in his own name! This "Glimpses" book I happen to be reading now was originally a present to my grandmother from Uncle John and Aunt Dorothy. Inscribed on the title page is "To dear Bea, wishing you many happy returns of your last birthday! Love J & D." (Roger Lancey)

Uncle Horace was special at first because of his name. So close to Horse. I learned that it was an old name in the family. He was a mirthful man and Aunt Annie a kind woman. They were rarely in Three Rivers but when they were, it was a BIG EVENT. With them came OLDER boy cousins! Horace was a man of jokes and pranks. Mother told me that when Aunt Annie and Uncle Horace's first child was born and died at birth – Margaret was her name – Uncle Horace was furious with the doctor. (Alice Wickenden MacEwen)

Uncle Horace, I met him only once; he had a great sense of humour . . . a bit of a devil . . . but a delightful man, as were his sons Roddy and Mack. (John French Wickenden)

With Horace it was almost continuous fun. At the airport meeting me, we looked at another very large man descending the stairs. "He could never travel light, could he?" quipped Horace. Later I realized that he and John had a great relationship through their letters, the main form of contact in those days, always finding amusing stories to pass on to each other. (Roger Lancey)

Horace had A NOSE. Annie had a small nose. She told me that when there were teasings among the French children about the noses of some of them, her mother (my Grandma French) would say, "Horace's nose suits Horace's face and Annie's nose suits Annie's face." (Alice Wickenden MacEwen)

When you needed your engagement ring, you got in touch with Uncle Horace, who told you who to get in touch with in Montreal. (Harriet Wickenden Taylor)

Charlotte Muriel Mabel ("Lottie") French, 1891-1980

Lottie was the second-youngest of the siblings. Excerpts from her obituary paint a summary picture of her life that began in Scotstown, continued in Winnipeg and Montreal, before returning to Cookshire in retirement:

> Lottie Muriel Mabel French was born July 23, 1891 at Scotstown . . . She received part of her education at the Cookshire Academy. The family moved to Winnipeg [*actually, the **family** moved to Humboldt, Minnesota*] where she finished her education, obtaining a teacher's diploma from the Winnipeg Collegiate Institute, and taught at Swan River for a number

Lottie French - 1916

Left: Lottie French, 1916 (courtesy of Ken Watson)
Above: Malcolm and Lottie Mackenzie, ca. 1951 (courtesy of Leslie Buckle)

Ellen French's house on Craig Street, Cookshire, ca. 1958 (photo by author)

L-R: John French, Dorothy French, Malcolm Mackenzie, Ron Buckle, Leslie Buckle, Lottie Mackenzie; Beaconsfield, Que., 1961 (courtesy of Leslie Buckle)

Lottie and Malcolm Mackenzie, Cookshire, July 1966 (courtesy of Roger Lancey)

of years. She met her husband-to-be, Malcolm Kenneth Mackenzie, of Plaister Mines, N. S., in Winnipeg, and they were married on August 28, 1918, in St. Peter's Church, Cookshire, and spent most of their married life in Montreal West, where she was active in the Women's Club. After her husband retired from work in the Dominion Bridge Company, they came to live in Cookshire in 1965. (*Sherbrooke Daily Record*, May 8, 1980)

Niece Alice Wickenden MacEwen retains fond early memories of Lottie and Malcolm:

> Aunt Lottie was lovely. She was soft of speech, loving and patient; she had a sweet nature. Mother stayed in Montreal West at the Mackenzie home on Easton Avenue as she awaited each of us, save Jean. It was a fun home to visit; relaxed and welcoming always. There were all the "MACKENZIE GIRLS" too – who weren't my sisters – so different big girls. Staying there was a picnic, a treat.

> Uncle Malcolm was a gentle man. Martha says that he had a magic trick and could find a quarter behind her ear at a moment's notice. I remember that when he flew to Halifax, to Nova Scotia from whence he came, he kneeled and kissed the ground. HOME, AT LAST.

> In addition to their three daughters, Lottie and Malcolm also had a son, Rodney French Mackenzie, who died days after he was born. As Mother said, "It was so sad." (Alice Wickenden MacEwen)

After their return to Cookshire, Lottie and Malcolm's house (where Ellen and Pertie had lived and where generations of Baileys had lived before them) became a popular home base for visiting relatives, as indicated by the Record's social notes and first-hand visitor reports:

> Mr. and Mrs. Horace French have returned home to Wetaskiwin, Alta. , after spending two weeks, guests of Mr. and Mrs. M. Mackenzie. Other recent guests were Mr. and Mrs. John Wickenden, Three Rivers, Miss Leslie Buckle and three friends, Montreal. (*Sherbrooke Daily Record*, Oct. 12, 1968)

> That first evening of my July 1966 visit to Cookshire, we walked along Craig South to Number 315, where Lottie and her husband, Malcolm, were then living. (Roger Lancey)

> On my 1970 visit I stayed with Lottie and Malcolm. I mention in my diary that it was lovely to see them again and "poor Uncle John." [Dorothy had passed away only a few months earlier.] Lottie caused us all to laugh as she pointed out "these old octogenarians staggering about the place – the halt, the deaf and the blind . . ." John, whom one could certainly now describe as frail, Malcolm was very deaf, and Charlie Fraser (now 89, and visiting from along the road) was, indeed nearly blind! My last evening in Cookshire on that visit I described as "wonderful." An excellent meal with Lottie, Malcolm and John. (Roger Lancey)

> Once my grandparents [Lottie and Malcolm] moved to Cookshire, probably around 1966 or '67, they were very close to Uncle John and Aunt Dorothy, playing bridge a lot. I think all four of them were pretty good players. (Leslie Buckle)

My own siblings recall their visits to the Mackenzie household:

> Brother Stevens and I occasionally watched Montreal Canadiens hockey games on Saturdays in the 1960s at Mr. and Mrs. Mackenzie's home because the Frasers had no TV. Back then, the CBC did not start their telecasts until 8:30 p.m. and we always enjoyed viewing the last few minutes of "The Honeymooners" before Danny Gallivan and Dick Irvin came on. Mr. Mackenzie was a diehard, ardent and staunch Toronto Maple Leafs fan and often sparred vocally with Stevens. (Warren Fraser)

> I went to the Mackenzie's once or possibly twice in the mid to late 1960s with Steve and Warren to watch hockey on TV. They lived on Craig Street, beside the Demers family and across from the Bellams. I also delivered their mail in the late '60s or early '70s, and remember their daughters Margaret (Buckle) and Rhona (Ferguson). The Fergusons would come visit at least a couple times a year, during which time their daughter Laurie would spend a lot of time at our farm. We were about the same age; she was a beautiful girl, and I became very fond of her. I have often wondered how things could have evolved differently if the same means of communication existed back then as we have today, with cellular phones and social media. Although I didn't know Margaret well, I

would see her often in Cookshire in later years. She lived in the same house where her parents had lived. (David Fraser)

I recall visiting Lottie and Malcolm's home and meeting "Herman Munster," a green-complexioned, scar-faced fellow that talked when you pulled a string: witty comments like "I like picnics – in the graveyard" and "I eat spinach – for my complexion." (This was perhaps around 1968; the technology was ahead of its time!) For a few years in the early 1970s I delivered their mail on the way home from school. (Jim Fraser)

I remember Lottie Mackenzie. I am quite sure I went to her home with some of my brothers and Diane to watch a Canadiens hockey game on TV. (Karen Fraser Jackson)

Annie Eliza Catherine French, 1897-1991

And last – but certainly not least – there was Annie. I daresay this book would never have been written, were it not for **her** family, so to her I offer a special salute.

At a very early age, after the sudden death of her father, Annie's world was turned upside down when her mother had to move to Minnesota, taking her and Lottie with her. In spite of this, Annie not only survived, but apparently thrived, excelling at school there. When they returned to Cookshire in 1910, her academic success continued. Without further introduction, I will allow Alice – one of her five daughters – to tell you what kind of person Annie was:

> Now we come to Annie. She was sharp as a tack. Small and capable. She ruled!

Hampden, Minn. schoolhouse, ca. 1905 (courtesy of Ken Watson)

Annie French, Hallock, Minn., ca. 1910 (courtesy of Ken Watson)

Dearly beloved

My husband would say, "Your mother has a mind like a steel trap." That is no bad thing. We shared books and had a language all our own. I benefited from having her more to myself than the older girls. My Grandma French, Lottie and Annie, moved to Humboldt, Minn., after her father died. Family accounts give the years there as about 1905 to 1912.

When Mother moved back to Cookshire, she walked to school her first morning. She told me that a boy walked with her and asked, "Are you smart?" She demurred, then replied "Sort of." It happened that she knew no French and no Latin. At that, Mother said "[My teacher] Miss Macdonald took me in hand and every day after school taught me both." Need I say who came first at the end of the year in both subjects? What a tribute to both the teacher and the pupil. Mother told me she learned to read sitting beside someone reading The Sherbrooke Record who took the time or had the time to help her with the printed word. She deciphered the words "Sherbrooke Daily Record" and her reading life began.

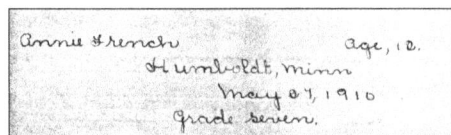

Annie French essay cover page, Humboldt, Minn., 1910 (courtesy of Alice Wickenden MacEwen)

Another memory: Mother and her best friend Hazel Sawyer would walk home after school and make a pan of fudge and then EAT IT ALL! "All of it?" I would ask. I think she allowed a "Yes." One Easter, her sister Lottie was given a chocolate egg. It was secreted away by Lottie; we know why. Mother found it and had a bite. Then another. Realizing there was no going back, she ate the whole thing! Lottie was not pleased.

In school, quoting Romeo and Juliet which the class was studying, a classmate arrived one day wearing a hand-me-down coat and said "You all do know this mantle." That has always stood out in my mind. I liked and like the wit of her words (and wore forever my sisters' mantles). As a child, Mother would visit friends and neighbours, and I daresay she was an engaging girl. She remembered that when she left, the farewell was "Don't be a stranger, Annie."

Mother's Big Brothers looked after her and the rest of the family as best they could after C. W. B. French died. She told me of the gifts that came from their ventures to Montreal, specifically, shoes for Annie. Uncle John called Mother "Chief" and I know it must have come from the fact that when Little Annie wanted something, she got it – indulged by her far older big brothers, Charles, John and Horace. And my dad picked up where they left off. Her brothers were revered by the six of us. (Alice Wickenden MacEwen)

Personally, I don't ever remember meeting Annie, although Alice remembers visiting my parents' farm in Cookshire with her mother (Annie). And my Grammy Fraser's diary notes a visit from Annie French on July 8, 1945. (I would have been only 18 months old at the time!)

> I know that Mother thought the world of your parents, your mother Alice, who cared for Donald's mother, bedridden for seven years, and of Donald, who would turn to Mother in class and whisper "French, French, what's the answer?" Mother would add, "Donald was so tired in school, he was up very early at the farm." (Alice Wickenden MacEwen)

Intrigued by this supposed exchange between Annie and my dad, I decided to investigate. I came up with the following interesting results (no pun intended):

- Cookshire Academy Results: II. Model – 1st prize, Annie French (*Sherbrooke Daily Record*, Oct. 7, 1911)
- Cookshire Academy Results: I. Academy – Annie French, 813; . . . Donald Fraser, 580 (*Sherbrooke Daily Record*, Aug. 5, 1913)
- Cookshire Academy Results: II. Academy – Annie French, 802; . . . Donald Fraser, 532 (*Sherbrooke Daily Record*, Aug. 14, 1914)

Not only was Annie an excellent academic student, but she was very interested in drama and literature, as illustrated by the following examples:

> The cast for a play to be presented at Cookshire includes Lucie Noble, Hazel Sawyer, Pattie Husbands, Marjorie Planche, Irene Chaddock, Annie French, Annie Cromwell and Gretchen Taylor. (*Sherbrooke Daily Record*, Oct. 30, 1914)

> DEPARTURES: Annie French to Macdonald College (*Sherbrooke Daily Record*, Jan. 10, 1916)

> COOKSHIRE: The play "The Camp Fire Girls" as given by the young ladies of Cookshire, under the direction of Miss Ruby Goff, was a great success. The scenery, costumes, singing and acting all far exceeded the expectations of the audience. The cast of characters was as follows: Peggy Malone, a little drudge, Evangeline Planche; Mrs. Bacon, a boarding house keeper, Georgie Learned; Beulah Marie, her daughter, aged 17, Annie French . . . The parts were all well taken, and in the rendering gave much evidence of musical dramatic ability . . . The total receipts for the play amounted to $150. (*Sherbrooke Daily Record*, Aug. 20, 1918)

> One of Annie's favourite expressions: "This winds up the fruitcake" (when something is completed). (Alice Wickenden MacEwen)

> I have beside me a poem that is ANNIE to me. She knew and resorted, when it was appropriate, to the written word. If we, walking in Trois-Rivières, passed a young man – weedy is the best description – holding up a lamp post, she would say, sotto voce, "O what can ail thee, Knight at Arms, Alone and Palely Loitering?" (Those are the opening lines of Keats' "La belle dame sans merci.") If there was a rush to get something or find something, she might say (and I followed suit), "She left the web, She left the loom, She made three paces through the room" and carry on with her favourite poem, Tennyson's "The Lady of Shalott." Yes, my childhood

was enriched! And the day I heard Dad recite Poe's "Annabelle Lee" or part of it, I was stunned. How could someone who lived, I thought, to build, know poetry? It did not fit. (Alice Wickenden MacEwen)

In December, 1923, Annie was married – once she had received the approval of key family members:

> Mother told me that when she went to Cookshire with Dad in tow TO MEET THE FAMILY; both brothers, Charlie and John, approved. (Alice Wickenden MacEwen)

> MARRIAGE: FRENCH – WICKENDEN: The marriage took place at noon on Saturday, in St. Peter's Church, Cookshire, of Annie, younger daughter of the late Mr. Charles French and of Mrs. French of Cookshire, to Mr. Jean François Wickenden, of Montreal, son of Mr. R. G. Wickenden, of Brooklyn, N.Y., the well-known artist, and Mrs. Wickenden. . . The bride, who was given away by her brother, Mr. John French, wore a gown of cocoa coloured georgette, with a hat of the same shade, and she carried a bouquet of butterfly roses. . . A reception was held after the ceremony at the residence of the bride's brother, Mr. John French, at Cookshire. . . (*Sherbrooke Daily Record*, Dec. 18, 1923)

Annie French and John Wickenden wedding photo, 1923 (courtesy of Alice Wickenden MacEwen)

Jocelyn Anne Wickenden (14 yrs), Martha Louise Wickenden (12 yrs), Catherine Jean Wickenden (17 yrs). Front = Alice Mary Wickenden (6 yrs), Harriet French Wickenden (8 yrs) & John French Wickenden (5 yrs)

Annie's six children (courtesy of Ken Watson)

Annie's husband, Jean François, had received a degree in Civil Engineering from McGill University a few months earlier. In 1928 he formed his own construction company, John F. Wickenden Co. Ltd. One of his career highlights was his success as President of the Bridge Committee in initiating the construction of a bridge across the St. Lawrence River, linking Trois Rivières with Sainte-Angèle on the

Laviolette Bridge, Trois-Rivières to Sainte-Angèle, Que. (wikipedia.org)

south shore. It was he (through my godfather) who gave me my first job – a summer job in 1964 working as a labourer on one of his company's construction projects in Shawinigan.

The marriage proved to be very fruitful, with five girls (Jocelyn, Jean, Martha, Harriet and Alice) and a single boy (John) joining the Wickenden household. Being the mother of six children, Annie obviously developed an impressive set of parenting skills, as illustrated by the following anecdote:

Jean-François Wickenden and grandnephew Roger Lancey beside new bridge construction, Trois-Rivières, July 1966 (courtesy of Roger Lancey)

> One morning, probably in 1943 or '44, I sang a new ditty to Mother before leaving for school. I remember the lyrics well and must have heard them hanging around the school yard!
> "YOU'RE IN THE ARMY NOW, YOU'RE IN THE ARMY NOW,
> YOU'LL NEVER GET RICH BY DIGGING A DITCH
> YOU SON OF A BITCH, YOU'RE IN THE ARMY NOW!"

Mother marched me into the living room where Dad was reading *The Gazette* and said, "SING THAT TO YOUR FATHER." I did. His only comment was "Don't sing it again." It must have been hard to keep a straight face and it was generous of them to appreciate the innocence of my rendering it. And that has nothing to do with Cookshire and the Frenches save that music was a way of life and our piano was where Mother sat and played. In World War II I remember lying in bed and listening to music and singing, young men's voices, Mother and Dad entertaining servicemen who were in Three Rivers before going overseas. (Alice Wickenden MacEwen)

As clearly demonstrated above, there was much love shared both among John and Dorothy's siblings and within their families. I can think of no better way to close this chapter than with a poem that epitomizes that love. The ode was penned by John French Wickenden, the youngest child of the youngest sibling.

Ode To Bonnie

There are strange things done
'Neath the midnight sun,
A borrowed phrase that you know;
And as I try to sleep tonight,
I can only think of you.
And I think of the many wonderful years
That we have shared together;
And of the faith you had in me,
And the dream of our life forever.

In this northern land, the Yukon vast,
There's a stillness that's hard to believe;
And the mountains and valleys, apart, yet near,
As are we in our love so dear.
And they meet every time in a valley stream,
Running endlessly to the sea.
So I think of you darling and I want you to know
You mean everything to me.

Without mountains and valleys
There'd be no streams;
Without rivers
There's be no sea.
You're my mountain, my valley,
My river and stream;
Thank you for loving me.

I love you

"Ode to Bonnie" (courtesy of John French Wickenden)

Chapter 10
A Special Kind of Family

Godparents are special because they are chosen. (author unknown)

Infant baptism clipart (clker.com); baptismal font at St. Peter's Church, Cookshire (photo by Linda Hoy)

Obituaries seldom tell the whole story. John French's published post-mortem piece was a case in point. It reads, in part "There were no children from this marriage . . ." Whoa! Stop! They **did** have children – and **lots** of them. I am referring, of course, to godchildren. This chapter describes how that family evolved and the special relationship that existed between the Frenches and their Fraser godsons and goddaughters.

Family of 14 . . . and counting

John and Dorothy's retirement years were even more fruitful than already described in Chapter 8. Concurrently with their many other activities, they were busy building a family. The first was a boy, Charles Ward Kenneth, who joined their family on July 30, 1936.

Then came a girl, Marina Alice, on June 17, 1939. Over the succeeding years, eleven more children were added. The final one was James Allan on August 11, 1957. And I must not forget to mention Martha, whom John had earlier brought into the family on October 19, 1930 – some five years before his marriage to Dorothy.

Yes, indeed, this caring couple were godparents to no less than 14 children – and quite likely even more. Their baptismal family included their niece Martha Wickenden, my cousin, Charles Fraser, as well as all my 11 siblings and myself. Interestingly, nine of us Frasers were baptized in batches of three. Why the other three were "done" individually remains a mystery. Perhaps it was because the priest who commanded the St. Peter's pulpit at the time was one who believed that unbaptized babies would end up in hell should they die. I was christened as part of the second Fraser threesome, as noted in my grandmother's 1947 diary entry:

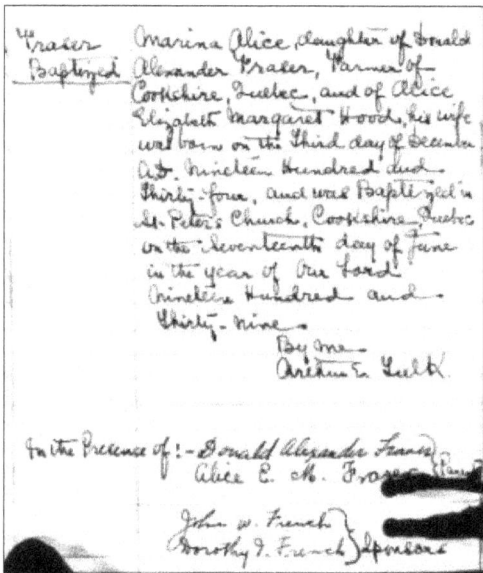

Charles W. K. Fraser baptism record, 1936 (ancestry.ca)

Marina Alice Fraser baptism record, 1939 (ancestry.ca)

Alice Fraser with her first Fraser "baptismal batch of 3" (Fraser family archives)

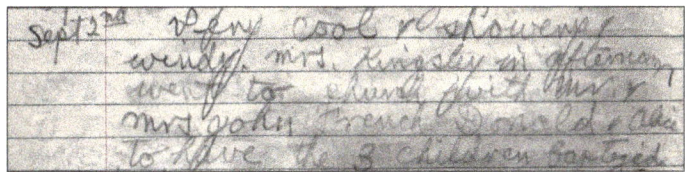

John and Dorothy French godparents at Malcolm, Winston and Marilyn baptisms (Lilla J. Fraser's diary, Sep. 2, 1947)

My three youngest siblings were christened as part of the final trio in August 1957:

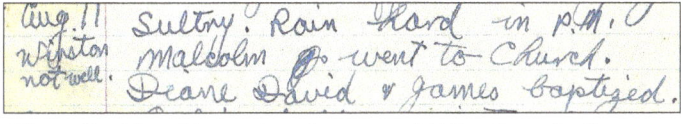

Diane, David and James baptisms noted (Alice Fraser's diary, Aug. 11, 1957)

The Fraser-French relationship

My family's relationship with John and Dorothy is an interesting one that is not easy to articulate. Although there was frequent contact between the Frenches and my parents (a study of my Mom's diaries over a 20-year period found the journals to be replete with French references – documenting more than 100 interactions), it would be a stretch to say that our families were close. In fact, one of my

The "Fraser 12" siblings, ca. 1965 (Fraser family archives)

younger brothers, David, questions why John and Dorothy were chosen to be our godparents:

> I question why they accepted to be our godparents; also why they were asked (godparents normally take an interest in the child's upbringing and personal development, and offer mentorship). I say this because I have no memories of them ever coming to visit Mom and Dad. (David Fraser)

Although the outward signs of a special relationship seemed to be missing, I firmly believe that my parents and the Frenches had a deep mutual love, respect and understanding. It is important to understand that, in those days, especially in some families, such emotions were not as openly expressed as today. Be that as it may, my siblings and I grew up with a healthy respect for our godparents.

Apart from knowing that our godfather was, for a brief time, a Member of the Quebec Legislative Assembly, we didn't see him or Dorothy as people who stood out from the crowd. In a 1997 article entitled "Colourful Citizens of Cookshire" published in our family newsletter *Fraser Family Link*, neither John nor Dorothy was mentioned among the almost 100 persons named in the piece. By contrast, all their close neighbours (see Chapter 12) made the list. Even Rodger Heatherington, who knew almost every English-speaking family in Cookshire, didn't really know them:

> When much younger, I delivered the *Sherbrooke Record* (daily) and the *Star Weekly* (weekly). I had over 140 clients for the *Star Weekly*, including most of the town's anglophones. However, I was never able to get the Frenches as clients so didn't get to know them as well as other residents whose homes I visited regularly. (Rodger Heatherington)

Although the Frenches might have lacked the charisma of their contemporary Cookshire-ites, they were far from invisible, both to our family and to the community at large, as detailed earlier in Chapter 8.

John and Dorothy were a frequent presence in my parents' lives, whether to assist with certain farm chores, to come bearing gifts or just to have a visit. Following are a few such interactions that made it into my mom's daily diary:

- 1949, May 16: John French brought pigs
- 1949, June 27: John French took kiddies for ride in PM
- 1949, July 24: John French for sing-song in evening
- 1950, June 12: John French brought chicks in evening
- 1950, Dec. 24: John French brought kiddies presents
- 1951, Aug. 8: John French brought puppy in PM
- 1953, Apr. 22: John French called to see baby Diane
- 1955, Sep. 25: Callers – Mr. & Mrs. John French
- 1957, Apr. 13: John French went to [sugar] camp

- 1960, Mar. 26: Winston at John French's to see TV in evening
- 1962, Apr. 16: Dad babysat & John French came

When asked what adjectives best described our godparents, my siblings and some family friends offered the following:

John: friendly, appreciative, forgiving, fair, kind, well-dressed, well-spoken, generous, a gentleman, sense of humour, man with a presence, straight shooting, honest, approachable, well-respected, stern, eagle-eyed, forceful.

Baby chicks (istockphoto; credit roman023)

Dorothy: pleasant, caring, slight, attractive, medium short, well-dressed, reserved, quiet, kind, classy, sophisticated, smiling, cheerful, a real lady.

My sister Marilyn remembers the Frenches' generosity:

> They would always buy a copy of whatever we were selling on behalf of the Junior Red Cross, whether it be Red Cross magazines or Red Cross calendars. (Marilyn Fraser Reed)

Hired helpers

Except for my two eldest sisters, all my siblings and I took our turns as the Frenches' hired helpers doing all kinds of housekeeping, grounds keeping and errand-running tasks. Following is a sampling as recorded verbatim in Mom's daily diaries from 1957 to 1970:

- 1957, Apr. 25: Boys helped John French in PM
- 1957, Oct. 26: Malcolm helped John French in PM
- 1959, Oct. 15: Malcolm worked at John French windows
- 1960, May 21: Winston worked all day for John French
- 1960, Aug. 1: Stevens & Warren helped John French in cemetery in afternoon
- 1960, Aug. 6: Winston worked at John French wood all day
- 1961, Sep. 26: Malcolm mowed John French lawn
- 1962, Oct. 20: Stevens working for John French
- 1968, Feb. 19: Warren worked for John French
- 1968, June 7: Warren mowed John French's lawn in AM
- 1968, Oct. 9: Warren worked for John French, he [John French] returned from hospital
- 1969, Feb. 5: David shovelled snow for John French

- 1969, Sep. 24: Karen helped John & Dorothy French
- 1969, Sep. 29: David worked for John French after school
- 1969, Nov. 29: Jimmy helping John French in PM
- 1970, Jan. 14: David shovelled at John French's after school

In the following personal anecdotes, several of my siblings recall both the challenges and rewards of working for their godparents:

> Sometime in 1969, I went to their home and did some work for them. To be honest, I can't remember exactly what the job was. It was perhaps dusting furniture or cleaning silver. (Karen Fraser Jackson)

> After brother Stevens graduated from high school and went to work at Bell, I took over delivering their mail six days a week. In the summer, I cut their lawn front and back, while John French would keep his eyes on me throughout the chore. In the winter, I shovelled snow from the long ascending cement steps from Craig Street to their porch. There were times when I had to (reluctantly) remove accumulated roof snow! (Warren Fraser)

Front steps to John French's Craig St. residence in winter, ca. 1960 (photo by author)

> I used to do the ironing for them, specifically John's shirts and pants. This could have been around 1967-68 though I am not certain of the dates. It was a learning experience for me. I had never, ever starched a shirt collar before, so Dorothy had to show me how. Even though I did ironing for Mom, I never ever starched anything, and I never had to press pants to perfection. I was a fast learner, and they paid me well. They were always very kind and pleasant. (Diane Fraser Keet)

Ironing board and iron (istockphoto; credit Michelle Gibson); shirts with starched collars (ohsospotless.com)

In the early days of autumn, John French wanted me to rake some leaves and then burn them. After wasting a few matches trying to ignite my big pile of damp leaves, I wandered into his shed and found a jug of lawnmower gasoline. "This will help," I thought, and proceeded to pour a considerable amount upon the leaves. Then I bent over and struck a match. "POOF!" and the pile totally scattered! My face burned, my eyebrows cooked, and the edges of my hair, below my hat, curled, BUT the leaves DID NOT burn! I pulled out my handkerchief and gently rubbed my sooty face. Then, rather tentatively, I knocked on John French's door and asked to use their bathroom (so I could scrutinize any facial damage). After cleaning up, but still red-faced, I sheepishly told John French that the leaves were too wet to burn. I accepted remuneration for the work done and biked home. (Warren Fraser)

Burning leaves (istockphoto; credit gyro); burnt face (istockphoto; credit OcusFocus)

I mowed their lawn for a summer or possibly two summers when I was in my very early teens (taking over from Warren when he left the area). I can't remember many details, but one time when I was mowing near the street, one of the wheels fell off. I ran over it, which made a loud noise and stopped the motor. I remember sobbing and expecting to be scolded by Mr. French, but their kind neighbour, Paul St-Laurent, immediately came to the rescue and comforted me, and then he either fixed or replaced the damaged wheel. I was so relieved! I also washed and helped install storm windows once, and it took me several attempts to remove all the streaks to John's satisfaction! (David Fraser)

Lawnmower with missing wheel (istockphoto; credit Andrii Borodai); cleaning windows (fallsafetyapp.com)

John French was a real stickler for how he wanted his grass cut. You had to do it first in one direction – say north-south – and then in the opposite direction – east-west – over the same area. This technique had to be followed exactly because he was sitting on the porch watching! (Steve Fraser)

Author's note: I found this façon-de-faire quite fascinating, so I decided to check whether there was any scientific rationale to justify the double-cutting. Well, in fact, there is:

Should I change direction each time I mow? Yes! Why? Because when grass is mowed in the same direction over and over, it's trained to lean one way. . . Also, mowing in just one direction makes the lawn look worn out over time. Ideally, grass stems should grow straight up and stand tall. Mowing in different directions helps make that happen. (blog.davey.com)

Grass-mowing pattern (blog.davey.com)

In Chapter 6 we discovered that, to his nieces and nephews, John French was not the stern, serious man that I and most of my siblings had known him to be. Except for my brother Warren, that is, who shares a story where he experienced a glimpse of our godfather's sense of humour:

One snowy winter afternoon after school, my tall strapping cousin, Frasier Bellam, and I (wee Warren) decided to engage in a friendly wrestling match at the lower end of John French's driveway in front of his garage. After a minute or so, Frasier lost his footing and tumbled to the snow-covered ground with Warren atop. We dusted ourselves off and proceeded to stroll to our homes. The following morning, when I delivered the Frenches' mail, John French said to me – straight-faced – that he and Dorothy were very upset with me for being such a mean bully. However, his frown soon turned to a broad smile as John explained that they had watched the entire Bellam/Fraser tussle from their kitchen window and it looked (to them) like David had defeated Goliath! (Warren Fraser)

David and Goliath (nbsfitness.net)

On a personal note

Personally, I considered John and Dorothy French to be like family. After all, for several years, as their regular mail-boy, I saw them practically every day. On my way to school, I would first go to the post office and collect their mail. I note that

Author's baptismal certificate (Fraser family archives)

Army surplus canvas haversack schoolbag (worldwarwonders.co.uk); vintage post office boxes and drawers (westernoutdoortimes.com)

their mailbox was no ordinary 4-inch square cubbyhole with a hinged door. No, it wasn't even a box at all. It was a drawer roughly the size of two Montreal telephone directories! After carefully emptying the contents into my army-surplus canvas haversack-cum-schoolbag, I would walk back to their home on Craig Street where Dorothy smilingly greeted me as John reclined on the kitchen couch, anxiously awaiting the *Montreal Gazette*.

This may be an appropriate time for me to make a confession with respect to The Gazette that I delivered every day. As a hockey fanatic, I would sometimes "borrow" the Sports section and take it with me to school before returning it with the next morning's issue. But one day, I got caught, not realizing that John was also a big hockey fan and that he too wanted to read about the Canadiens' latest exploits. Live and learn!

Chapter 11
Cookshire Homes on Main and Craig

A house without a garden or orchard is unfurnished and incomplete. – A. Bronson Alcott (American teacher and writer)

Neither John nor Dorothy was born in Cookshire, but both moved there some time following the passing of their respective fathers. This chapter focuses on their two postnuptial homes in the town. Both properties were defined in Eaton Township's historical cadastral records as "part of Lot 11 in the 8th range." They are shown in a vintage Town plan as lots 11-9 and 11-32.

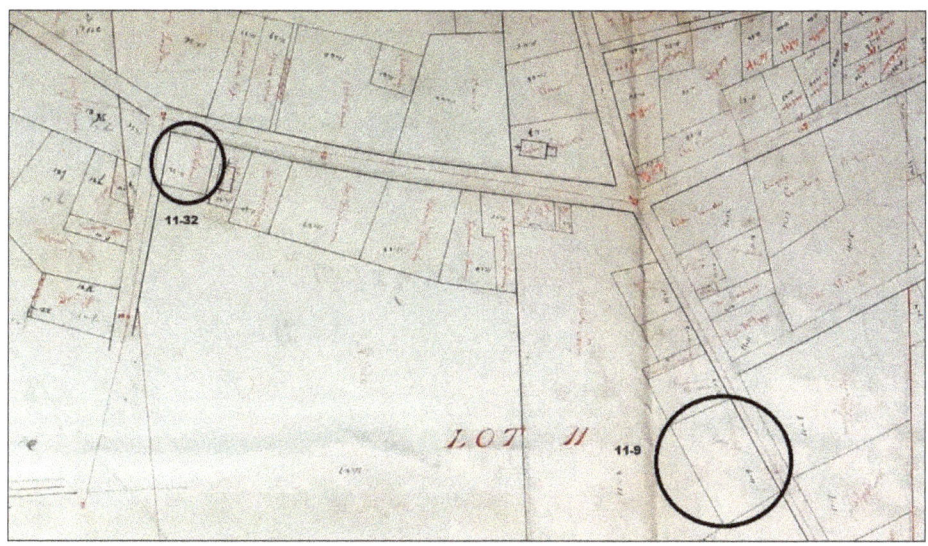

Cookshire lot plan showing Craig and Main streets with J. W. French properties circled (BANQ.qc.ca)

We will see that the two homes – the first on Main Street and the second on Craig Street – shared a number of common characteristics.
- a property that was pretty but not pretentious
- a home that was comfortable but not a castle
- gardens that were artistic but not artificial-looking
- outbuildings that were utilitarian but not eyesores

Obviously these two homes were both well-built since they still proudly stand as sentinels that have survived the shifting sands of time.

Maison-mère on Main

House of John Wellington French. Cookshire 1929

John French's first house, on Main Street (courtesy of Ken Watson)

Uncle John French - Cookshire (Kate McIver's house) - 1936

John in front of his Main Street house, 1936 (courtesy of Ken Watson)

The French's first family residence in Cookshire was at the top of Main Street, just past the United Church. John purchased the property in 1920, living there with his mother until her passing in 1933. He continued to live there following his marriage to Dorothy in 1935. The couple made this their home for the next 10 years.

The property's historical summary indicates that John bought the property in 1920 from the Learned family. He sold it some 25 years later, in August 1944, to Peter McDonald who, in turn, sold it five years after that to Colin Standish.

John French bought the property for the grand sum of $1500 and sold it a quarter century later for $6000.

John French's Main Street house (210 Main St. West) in 2020 (photo by David Fraser)

John and Dorothy's nieces recall various features of the home at the top of Main street:

Cadastral summary, John W. French Main Street property, Lot 11-32 (registrefoncier.gouv.qc.ca)

On this day the twenty fourth of January one thousand nine hundred and twenty. Before me: Ernest Lebrun Notary Public for the Province of Quebec residing and practising at the Town of Cookshire in the District of St. Francis. Came and appeared:-Mrs Alwilda Eoline Learned (née Fisher) presently of the said Town of Cookshire the widow of the late William Henry Learned, in his lifetime of the same place, accountant, her husband deceased, hereinafter called The Vendor, Of the One Part: And John W. French, of the same place Automobile dealer, hereinafter called the purchaser: Of the Other Part:) Which said vendor for the consideration hereinafter mentioned did and doth hereby sell convey and make over with warranty against all troubles and causes of eviction and free and clear of and from any and all incumbrances unto the said Purchaser present and accepting: Those certain tracts or parcels of land lying and being in the said Town of Cookshire, in the Township of Eaton, known on the Cadastral Plan and Book of Reference for the said Town of Cookshire as the lot number Eleven thirty two, (11-32) in the Eighth Range of the said Township of Eaton, containing sixteen thousand eight hundred feet in superficies, and the lot number eleven, one, one, (11-1-1) in the said Eighth Range of the said Township and containing five thousand eight hundred and eighty eight feet in superficies, together with the buildings and improvements thereon made and erected. As the whole is actually without any exception or reserve and belonging to the said vendor the said land and premises under and by virtue of the last will and testament of the late William Henry Learned, her husband deceased and registered in the Compton County Registry Office under No. 28728 as it appears in her delaration according to Article 2098 of the Civil Code for the Province of Quebec, also registered in the said Compton County Registry Office under No. 28729. to have and to hold the said hereby sold land and premises together with all and singular the rights members and appurtenances thereunto belonging or in any wise appertaining unto the said Purchaser, his heirs and assigns as his and their absolute property henceforth and forever and to enter upon and being already in possession of the same. The present sale is thus made for and in consideration of the price or sum of Fifteen hundred dollars which the said vendor doth hereby acknowledge to have had and received from the said Purchaser whereof quit. Whereof Acte. Done and passed at the said Town of Cookshire under the number two thousand nine hundred and ninety, three of the minutes of the undersigned Notary. And after these presents were duly read the said parties signed them with me the said Notary. Signed) Mrs A. E. Learned, John W. French, E. Lebrun, Notaire. True copy of the original minute remaining of record in my office. E. Lebrun, Notaire.

John W. French's Main Street property deed, Jan. 24, 1920 (registrefoncier.gouv.qc.ca)

Their first home that I knew – I remember walking straight into the kitchen from outside. It was a large kitchen; life was lived there. It had a couch or sofa in it so Uncle John could nap, I was told. And leading away from the house was a succession of sheds and butternut trees! (Alice Wickenden MacEwen)

"Uncle John's house" – so familiar that I can almost smell it. A walk into the kitchen showed to the left along the wall an open cupboard displaying dishes. On the immediate right and along that wall was a cozy couch or daybed – perhaps somewhere for Grandma (or Uncle John) to nap. I imagine things being baked in a wood stove required more attention than is given today using gas or electricity, so the cot would provide some welcome respite. (Martha Wickenden MacKellar)

I remember stepping out the door to the garden, marveling at the flowers. There were sweet Williams, the name was so different to what I knew and the flowers precious in appearance. I think there were cosmos too. (Alice Wickenden MacEwen)

The gardens in Cookshire – it was there that I first saw Sweet Peas, ENJOYED their sweet scent and delicacy of form. I have a vision of Aunt Dorothy in the garden so I imagine she did that as well as meals, laundry and provisioning. (Martha Wickenden MacKellar)

Uncle John French, Catherine Jean Wickenden (in costume), Aunt Dorothy French (Dorothy Isabella MacLeod) - 1936

John and Dorothy with niece Jean in garden of Main Street home, 1936 (courtesy of Ken Watson)

Sweet peas (pinterest.com); sweet Williams (siskiyouseeds.com)

John W. French's Craig Street residence, ca. 1960 (photo by author)

Classy compound on Craig

John and Dorothy's final Cookshire residence was an attractive rambling two-storey clapboard house prettily perched on a small incline above Craig Street. This acre-and-a-half property has a very interesting pedigree, as illustrated by its cadastral summary on the following page.

Although not indicated in the summary, John French's mother (and presumably John as well) lived in the Craig Street house for some period of time, ending in 1917 (when the Wilkinsons moved in) according to a reference in the *Sherbrooke Daily Record*. Perhaps the Frenches were renters of the property.

> NOTES
> Mr. and Mrs. John Wilkinson expect to move into their own house on Craig street shortly, which is at present occupied by Mrs. C. B. French.

Wilkinsons move to Craig Street
(*Sherbrooke Daily Record*, Apr. 28, 1917)

Dearly beloved

Cadastral summary of John W. French Craig Street property, Lot 11-9 (registrefoncier.gouv.qc.ca)

A fascinating summary of the property's owners, as seen through the eyes of the old oak tree that dominated the front yard, is contained on the Nadeau Family page of the *Cookshire 1892-1992* centennial book. (Daniel Nadeau purchased the property following the deaths of John and Dorothy in 1970.)

View of Craig Street house in 1893 (Cookshire 1892-1992)

If you carefully cock your ear under the old oak tree beside the entrance to 140 Craig Street South, you will receive lots of information through the light rustling of its leaves. As it leans over the house, its branches glancing at the vegetable garden that extends over the property's northwest slope, the 100-year-old tree will tell you about the English engineer who established a homestead here after marrying a local girl around 1893. It will also tell you how the farmer Goodwin settled here for a few years before turning the property over to English photographer John Wilkinson in 1902.

How many pictures did he take on the large verandah, under the pines or the butternuts, under the shade of the crooked willow or simply in the flower garden of a thousand varieties? Only the old oak has the answer. Neither is it surprising to see the property passed to a close relative from Belgium. His wife, a "pure laine" Englishwoman, enjoys having afternoon tea under the trees surrounded by the fragrance of flowers and the country calm. All the while, until 1936, her husband teaches in Lennoxville.

Then in 1944, the Wilkinson family sells the property to a retired wood merchant. John Wellington French enjoys having a few cows, some hens and a horse while the gentle Dorothy Isabella expertly tends to the flower and vegetable gardens that surround the house.

Finally, since 1970, the Nadeau family proudly maintains the flower gardens of a thousand scents in the east and a plentiful vegetable garden in the west. Furthermore, as if the old oak were to suggest to all the occupants it had seen pass, the many types of trees are always considered as true friends. (*Cookshire 1892-1992*, translated by author)

As mentioned above, John French purchased the Craig Street property in 1944. The purchase price was $16,000.

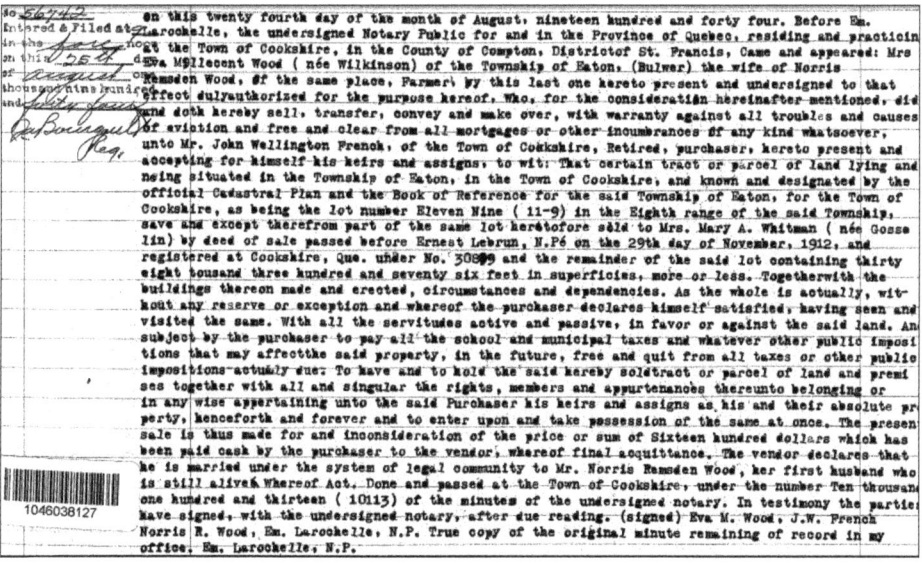

John W. French Craig Street property deed, Aug. 24, 1944 (registrefoncier.gouv.qc.ca)

Family and friends share their recollections of the property – the house, the outbuildings and the grounds:

> What I remember best was when we used to go to Cookshire when I was a child, probably from the age of about four to perhaps 15 or 16, we would stay at Uncle John and Aunt Dorothy's. I remember the house, particularly the long drive leading up to the garage, the chickens that Uncle John kept (that he referred to as "banties"), and the lovely "English" flower garden that you looked out onto from the verandah. I think it is referred to as an English garden because of the tall flowers in it, like phlox and hollyhocks. The house also had a special "old house" smell.

I can't describe it but I remember last summer staying at an old inn in the Rideau Lakes area close to Ottawa, and it had the same smell, that took me back to Cookshire. (Leslie Buckle)

My brother David and I, seven and nine years old respectively, had never been to a home like theirs before. I, for one, was truly enchanted! I recall a large, beautiful home, with a grand driveway, massive trees and the welcoming warmth and charm of both Uncle John and Aunt Dorothy. ... I remember being encouraged to explore their home and grounds there. The upper room where David and I stayed seemed to have been sort of an attic made up to welcome us. I recall quite a rain and windstorm occurred one night made the room and the window with swaying trees outside the stuff of children's books – which left one of us scared spitless during the storm! Not sure if it was my brother or me, but our parents were nearby and Aunt Dorothy's calm was reassuring. (Margie French)

John French relaxing on porch of his Craig Street house, 1947 (courtesy of Ken Watson)

They lived in a nice secluded house on a hill, surrounded by lots of trees, shrubs and flowers, with an impressive cement stairway from the front entrance of the house down to the street. (David Fraser)

I used to ride my bike around the French's driveway with Louis Jacques (who lived with his mother, Barbara Jacques and grandmother, Mrs. Fuller) across the road from the John French home. There was a large barn at the top of John's property and a garage just as you accessed the driveway from Craig Street. A small stream flowed alongside the southern portion of his property and driveway, between the French property and Charlie Fraser's property. It never completely dried up so I assume it was spring-fed from a source further up in the old Kirby farmland, owned by Isidore Doyon in my time. (Almon Pope)

I have several wonderful memories: the wrap-around porch, the babbling brook, the most beautiful flower garden and the wood stove in the kitchen. Maybe 15 years ago, my father, my step-mother and my son took a vacation to Canada. We got to visit my grandmother's grave and actually stopped by my aunt's home. The flower garden was still there. The owner happened to be outside, and I was able to speak with her for a minute. I was surprised that the farm behind them was now a development. It was always so cool to see cows outside their window in the kitchen, since I grew up in the suburbs. (Kathi Kressman)

I remember Dorothy had a number of bantam chickens that scurried through her flower beds. As a child I loved to watch them. (Muriel French Fitzsimmons)

It was a beautiful home with a welcoming front verandah. I mowed their lawn a couple of times. (Charles W. K. Fraser)

Among the most engaging characteristics of the property were the lawns and gardens. Gorgeous flower beds decorated every corner and contour.

Flower gardens at John and Dorothy's Craig Street home, ca. 1960 (photos by author)

Dorothy obviously was blessed with a very green thumb, but she also had a bit of help from the Frasers in nurturing and maintaining her Garden of Eden. My mom's diary mentions that we provided both manual and manure support. It also recorded a lightning strike that victimized a tree on the grounds – perhaps it was the old oak tree that narrated the property's history earlier in this chapter.

- May 1, 1950: Dad took one load manure to John French
- May 22, 1962: Winston put in John French garden
- May 30, 1968: Thunderstorms struck John French's tree (Alice Fraser's diaries)

According to the recollections of family, friends and Fraser siblings, the house's interior had many nice features:

I remember it being a very beautiful home! (Karen Fraser Jackson)

> How bright and light it was inside! (Rodger Heatherington) *Author's note: That is probably because the house had so many windows – seemed like 100 windows when I was hired to wash them all!*
>
> I remember their home being tidy and well-kept. (Doris Pope)
>
> Every room was very spacious, beautifully arranged and, as my mother would say, "everything was in its place." It was real homey. (Dorothy Ross)
>
> I was only ever just inside the front door, so I recall very little, but I think it had a lot of nice woodwork. (Jim Fraser)
>
> I was in their large kitchen on hundreds of occasions, as I always delivered their mail at the side door off the long driveway. (Warren Fraser)

The house was nicely furnished. Following John's and Dorothy's passing in 1970, two special pieces of furniture found new homes. Members of the recipients' families describe the heirlooms and their ultimate destinies:

> My mum [niece Jocelyn Wickenden Watson] loved Uncle John's secretarial desk because, as a child, she was fascinated by all its nooks and crannies that she was allowed to explore. When Uncle John died, she asked for the desk and was given it. I remember that it came to us black with age and character. Mum had it refinished and while it remained beautiful – and was probably even more beautiful because it had been refinished – I missed what it **had** been. Sadly, it was among the treasures we sold last summer – because we couldn't hang onto it any longer. (Mary Watson)
>
> John and Dorothy bequeathed their dining room set (table, six chairs and china cabinet) to Mac [Malcolm Fraser]. We were living in an apartment

Secretary desk similar to Uncle John's desk (courtesy of Mary Watson); John and Dorothy French's Jacobean dining room set (photo by David Fraser)

in the Pope Residence at that time. Without enough space to accommodate more furniture, we put the set in storage. In 1974, when we moved to Craig Street South, we installed the set in one end of the living room as a dining area. (Janice Fraser)

Author's note: When Mac and his second wife, Doreen, moved to Pine Hill Farm in 1989, the Frenches' Jacobean dining room set was brought with them, and it remains there to this day.

Dearly beloved

Chapter 12
Nearby Neighbours

A good neighbour – a found treasure. – Chinese proverb

John and Dorothy French were blessed with an eclectic company of Craig Street neighbours. This chapter consists of a roll call of the *homo sapiens* living nearest to them.

The Morrows

Within spitting distance (please pardon such an unsanitary metaphor!) were Andrew and Bernice Morrow, whose house bordered to the north. It is safe to say they were John and Dorothy's closest neighbours, both geographically and relationally.

Neighbours Andrew (Andy) and Bernice Morrow; the Morrows' house (courtesy of Bruce Learned)

Andy was a very upstanding (both figuratively and literally) citizen of Cookshire, having served multiple terms as mayor. Initially a farmer, then a carpenter, he later worked for Wallace Silversmiths and for the Maine Central Railroad. During his retirement he was frequently spotted sitting on the Frenches' porch, where he and John enjoyed talking politics or just shooting the breeze.

What I remember most about Andy Morrow was his height and his posture – he seemed seven feet tall and walked straight as a dye. Some of my siblings also recall these characteristics of his physique:

> Andy Morrow would bend slightly backwards when he stood and walked. (David Fraser)

Andy Morrow stood tall and was rather slim. (Warren Fraser)

A former neighbour of the Morrows' daughter remembers other aspects of his character:

> Andy Morrow was the kindest, most soft spoken man. He was the father of Mildred Learned, our next door neighbour. (Stanley Parker)

The Frasers/Frasiers

Immediately to the south of the Frenches were the adjacent properties of brothers Charlie Fraser and Jim Frasier. (Yes, these two brothers spelled their family name differently – but that's another story that is told in one of my earlier books, *OHIXIHO*.) Charlie and Jim were my dad's first cousins.

John W. French's Craig Street residence, with John French and Andy Morrow on the porch, 1960 (photo by author)

Charlie's residence was called "Maplemount" as it featured a long row of large sugar maples along the edge of the property. A confirmed lifelong bachelor, he lived there with his unmarried sisters. Charlie was intelligent and eccentric. A true jack-of-all-trades, he was variously a prospector, an inventor, a collector and a mathematician. His day job was chief chemist at the Frasier, Thornton & Co.

Charlie Fraser with his bicycle, ca. 1965 (photo by author)

Left: Charlie Fraser's "Maplemount" residence (courtesy of Charles W. K. Fraser)
Right: Charlie Fraser's "OHIXIHO" residence (photo by author)

patent medicines factory on Railroad Street in Cookshire. In many ways, Charlie was far ahead of his time – he was a fitness fanatic who travelled everywhere by bike since he never owned an automobile.

In 1958 Charlie moved the Maplemount property's carriage house onto the

James A. Frasier residence, "The Evergreens," 1991 (courtesy of Frasier Bellam)

open field next to the French property and converted it into his new residence, which he named OHIXIHO. In 1962 the stately Maplemount house was donated to Sherbrooke's Grace Chapel church group that converted it into a group home for young folk. The building was demolished several decades later following a fire.

Just south of Maplemount was Jim and Estelle Frasier's attractive estate "The Evergreens." Jim was president of Frasier, Thornton & Co.

The Fullers and the St-Laurents

Directly across Craig Street from John and Dorothy's house was the Bob Fuller residence. Originally known as the Wilford House, the "loggia" style building, constructed in 1820, was the first post office in Cookshire. The building is still standing today – 200 years later.

Family and friends share memories of the Fullers:

> Bob Fuller worked at Wallace Silversmiths where Dad worked, and was known to everyone in Cookshire. (Stanley Parker)

Wilford house on Craig Street, Cookshire, ca. 1896 (*History of Compton County*)

Bob Fuller drove a '37 Ford; he was retired and had a son Nelson; his home had a recessed veranda upstairs. (Charles W. K. Fraser)

I will never forget the valuable lesson that Mr. Bob Fuller taught me one spring, more than 50 years ago. Mr. Fuller wanted a "good" path cleared through the heavy snow so he could walk, using his cane, from his house opposite John French's to the small brook enroute to Mrs. Pennoyer's, in order to witness the beginnings of spring. I shovelled a bit in the morning on the way to school and I shovelled some more at noon, and then after school, I shovelled still more. I shovelled on Monday and on Tuesday and on Wednesday. When I finally finished on Thursday, I knocked on his door with great anticipation. Mr. Fuller came out, inspected the job and said how pleased he was. And he rewarded me with five pennies! I know that I should have been grateful, but I was expecting a bit more. But what a lifetime lesson – to agree on compensation first so there would be no consternation later! (John Fraser, extract from *Fraser Family Link*, July 1997)

House at 145 Craig St. South in 1992 (*Cookshire 1892-1992*)

Bob Fuller made up a rhyme, as [my cousins] June, Marina and John would often stop in:

> Junie and Johnny were hunting for flies
> Junie gave Johnny a pair of black eyes
> Junie asked Johnny if he wanted any more
> And Johnny said "No, my eyes are too sore" (Charles W. K. Fraser)

After the Fullers moved, the house became the property of Paul St-Laurent. Others share their recollections of the St-Laurents.

> Paul St-Laurent and his wife were very kind and generous people. I also knew their son Marc (who became a work colleague) and one of their daughters, Diane (I had a crush on her in the late 60's, but at the time I was much too shy to talk to her!). (David Fraser)

> I remember Paul St-Laurent and his father coming to "The Evergreens" to trim dead branches from some of our many trees. What was amazing about this was that they brought only a couple of axes each, but no saws. The axes were obviously very sharp, as were the skills of both father and son, each of whom, with two or three swings of an axe, would take out a chunk of wood the size of a fist, and with one or two more strikes, would bring down a branch the size of their forearm. (Frasier Bellam)

The Bourgaults

Neighbour Albert Bourgault house on Craig Street (Google maps)

Adjacent to the Fuller/St-Laurent property was the house of Monsieur Albert Bourgault, Compton County registrar. This residence was unique among the Frenches' neighbours, in that it was of much more recent construction than the surrounding older heritage homes. It also had the distinction of being the childhood home of one of Quebec's most famous independence advocates, Pierre Bourgault. Although Pierre lived in Cookshire when he was a child, he was away at boarding school for most of his youth. Only much later did he become involved in the Quebec independence movement.

Family and friends share their memories of Monsieur Bourgault:

> Monsieur Bourgault worked at county building. (Charles W. K. Fraser)

> Monsieur Bourgault was a well-known, competent notary and did some legal work for Dawn and me at the time of our marriage. (Stanley Parker)

> Pierre's Papa walked with a cane and would ALWAYS acknowledge my "Hello" with a nod of his head and a faint, "Allô." (Warren Fraser)

When Monsieur Bourgault put his insurance agency up for sale, I tried unsuccessfully to buy it, but he sold it to Lionel Pope. (Rodger Heatherington)

In his 2007 biography "BOURGAULT," author, Cookshire native and onetime Craig Street neighbour, Jean-François Nadeau tells the story of the Bourgaults' arrival in Cookshire:

> In Cookshire, in the 1940s, two societies [francophones and anglophones] lived side by side but without really knowing each other. . . sometimes the relations between the two communities became aggressive. When the St-Laurent family, neighbours of the Bourgaults, arrived, they remember being heckled by anglophones in an effort to scare them away. *[Author's note: Whatever animosity that may have existed, obviously dissipated over the years because Paul St-Laurent was a pallbearer at both Dorothy's and John's funerals in 1970.]*

Postcard of original County Building, Cookshire, ca. 1910 (courtesy of David Laberee)

When the Bourgaults arrived in Cookshire in January 1943, they were forced to stay in a hotel . . . because, according to Monsieur Bourgault, nobody wanted to sell him a house. . . However, many years later, Pierre said that the real reason was that there were no houses available. . . After renting a house at the top of Main Street *[This may, in fact, have been the house that John and Dorothy French vacated in 1944]*, Albert Bourgault decided to build his own house on a plot of land at the corner of Craig and Plaisance streets that he bought from Dr. Aurèle Lepine for $800 cash. The new house, all in wood, had only a single floor with a gentle sloped roof. The home was simple but cozy. (Jean-François Nadeau)

Pierre Bourgault on cover of book BOURGAULT by Jean-François Nadeau (luxediteur.com)

Other neighbours

Within a stone's throw or two from John and Dorothy's home (but in opposite directions) were the Pennoyers and the Rousseaus.

Nearby Neighbours

I still vividly recall two childhood incidents involving Mrs. Pennoyer (I assume she had a first name, but to us kids she was just "Mrs. Pennoyer.") In any case, on my way home from school one fine spring day, I spotted some beautiful lilies-of-the-valley just beyond the fence on the edge of her property. As I bent down and began picking a bouquet to take home to my mom, Mrs. Pennoyer came charging out of her house and practically read me the Riot Act. Needless to say, I didn't repeat that well-meaning gesture.

Dragging Christmas from Fraser woods, ca. 1958 (photo by author)

A few years later, in December, Mrs. Pennoyer called my mom to ask whether I could bring her a Christmas tree. So I went to my dad's woods, trudging across the frozen fields, to find her the perfect tree. I found a well-shaped tree and dragged it about a mile to her house. Arriving at her door, thinking that my mission was accomplished, I was taken aback when she rejected the tree, declaring that it was too small and not bushy enough. Undaunted, I dragged the tree back home and returned to the woods. After a half-hour of searching, I spotted just what the doctor ordered. So I cut it down and set out on the trek back to Mrs. Pennoyer's. Expecting this to be a triumphant conclusion to a fatiguing exercise, I was devastated when she once again declared it to be unacceptable. She wanted a balsam instead of a spruce. So back to the woods a third time I went, found a beautiful balsam and delivered it. This time she was finally satisfied and rewarded my efforts with a shiny new 25-cent piece! In retrospect, perhaps her lack of generosity was retribution for stealing her lilies-of-the-valley years before!

Just down the street from the Morrows were the Rousseaus. A former Cookshire resident fondly remembers Evariste:

> Another neighbour, just two houses down, was Evariste Rousseau. He worked at Osgood's store, where I worked one summer in '50 or '51 and also at Christmas time while at Bishop's University. He was a gem to work for. He taught me how to sweep the floor without wearing the broom down on one side! (Stanley Parker)

A bit further away, but still within easy walking distance, was Allie Pope's store on the corner of Craig and Main streets. Allie's grandson, Almon, reminisces:

> Both Mom and I remember John French being a best friend to my grandfather (Allie Pope). Allie would walk up to his house often for visits where they would most likely talk business or school board issues. Mom remembers John would come to the store where Allie and he would talk

Allie Pope's store, Cookshire (courtesy of Almon Pope)

Wilkinson's photo studio, Cookshire (Eastern Townships Resource Center)

> politics and, come election time, a group of the regulars would congregate and engage in conversation. Knowing the regulars at the store, I would suggest these gentlemen as possibly being involved: John "Johnny" McNally, Leon Desruisseaux, Edward ("Eddie") Baker, Frank Woolley, Stan McVetty and Cecil Gilbert. There were others but these would have had prolonged visits. I remember them and enjoyed listening in, having worked at the store after school hours and on weekends. (Almon Pope)

The other main gathering place for the English-speaking folk of Cookshire was the Dew Drop Inn, where John would occasionally "drop in." One such visit in 1959 was noted in my cousin's diary:

> Nov. 7, 1959: John F. [French] in for quite a while. (Mabel Fraser McVetty's diary)

The Wilkinson Brothers

Because John Wilkinson was the former owner of John and Dorothy's Craig Street property and because the Wilkinson Bros. Photo Studio was located just around the corner on Plaisance Street, it was felt appropriate to include them in this chapter. The Eastern Townships Resource Center provides an historical summary:

> The Wilkinson Brothers Studio opened in the spring of 1892. John Wilkinson (born in Scotland) and his brother, Alfred (born in Belgium) bought the studio of H. H. Weeden in Cookshire and reopened it under its new name. John had visited Canada and the United States from 1884 to 1885, and after completing his studies at the London Polytechnic School of Photography, he had returned in 1891 to settle in Cookshire with his brother. The Wilkinson Brothers were known to photograph both the upper and lower classes of the region, and they also contributed to the illustration of L.S. Channell's work, *History of Compton County*, published in 1896. John Wilkinson married Millicent Botterill. Alfred Wilkinson married Ethel Bigland. . . Records suggest Alfred left the photographic studio and served as headmaster at Bishop's College School in Lennoxville from 1911 to 1931. John continued to operate the photography studio without his brother into the 1930s. John died in Cookshire in 1946. (townshipsarchives.ca)

On the following page are two Wilkinson Bros. portraits with special connections to John and Dorothy French.

Even though John Wilkinson moved his residence to Craig Street in 1917, his photo studio remained on Plaisance Street. His great-grandson explains:

> I don't believe that the photo studio ever left Plaisance Street. I had occasion to visit the studio building with my Uncle David Wood (brother of my mother) and was exposed to remnants of the studio. (Jim Hurd)

Two Wilkinson Bros. portraits. Left: Mildred Morrow Learned (ETRC-P228-001-001_14_141); right: Annie French (courtesy of Alice Wickenden MacEwen)

Chapter 13
Resting in Peace "Up on the Hill"

The graveyard can be a place to bring the joy of rebirth and renewal to the spirit and wish our loved ones well on their onward voyage. – Angela Abraham (English author)

Gravestone of John and Dorothy French, Cookshire Cemetery (photo by author)

John and Dorothy both passed away, six months apart, in 1970. John's obituary noted that those six months were lonely ones for him:

> Mrs. French predeceased her husband on May 23, 1970, and the past six months he has sadly missed her bright smile and devoted companionship. (*Sherbrooke Record*, Dec. 9, 1970)

John and Dorothy's final resting place is in Cookshire Cemetery. This plot of land, located high above the Eaton River Valley about a mile out of town, is not your normal cemetery. No, it is unique and much of that uniqueness can be attributed to the French family and to John's lifelong association with the place, as acknowledged in his obituary:

> His contribution to the improvement of the Cookshire Cemetery was greatly appreciated by all who knew him, and is a fine monument to his efforts. (*Sherbrooke Record*, Dec. 9, 1970)

Dearly beloved

In the beginning

A look at the history of Cookshire Cemetery reveals the unusual nature of this burial ground. In Quebec, cemeteries were traditionally located in the centre of the village, were closely associated with parish churches of a specific religious denomination, and were often right in the churchyard itself. But Cookshire's cemetery is decidedly different. Because it is situated outside of town in a quiet, secluded field, there is nothing that threatens the perfect peace that permeates this place. It is indeed a holy place set apart for ever. Here lay the remains of Roman Catholics, Protestants, anglophones and francophones – all in peaceful cohabitation.

So how did this come about? It wasn't always that way. Cookshire's cemetery was initially located in the centre of town on a lot situated between Main and Plaisance streets. The land had been acquired from John Bailey in 1886:

> Deed of Sale executed by John C. Bailey, farmer, of Eaton aforesaid, to them as "The Cookshire Union Cemetery Company" and passed before Joseph J.Mackie, notary, on the twenty fifth day of May last [1886], of a certain lot or parcel of land containing about ten acres in superficies and forming part of lot number eight, in the ninth range of lots in said Eaton, to be used as a cemetery for ever. (*Official Gazette of Quebec*, July 24, 1886)

Alas, the "for ever" mentioned in the above Deed of Sale would **not** be for ever. Less than 20 years later, in 1904, the cemetery was moved:

> The [original] cemetery was moved to make place for a new [Roman Catholic] church whose construction began on June 24, 1904 and ended in 1905. The remains of the 244 persons buried here had to be moved to the current [new] cemetery. Those whose gravestones were still legible and in good condition were re-interred under their own gravestones; the others were reburied under the large cross. The [new] cemetery was blessed on October 25, 1908. (*Cookshire 1892-1992*)

The Official Gazette of Quebec formally announced the transfer of the former cemetery property to the Saint-Camille Roman Catholic parish:

> The Cookshire Union Cemetery Company will request the Lieutenant-Governor in Council, to obtain authorization to yield to the parish of Saint-Camille de Cookshire, the plot of land currently being used for the interment of Roman Catholics. (*Official Gazette of Quebec*, Aug. 1, 1908)

The new cemetery faced important financial challenges during its early years:

> MEETING OF COOKSHIRE CEMETERY ASSOCIATION: The question of finances was introduced and the secretary, Mr. C. MacRae reported no funds on hand, and several lot-owners in arrears. It was thought advisable to sell as many lots as possible, and to raise the price of same. .

. Mrs. George Cook, president of the Cookshire Homemakers' Club, read a resolution whereby the Homemakers' Club undertakes to establish . . . a Co-operative Cemetery Fund . . . for the upkeep of the Cookshire Protestant Cemetery. (*Sherbrooke Daily Record*, Nov. 4, 1919)

In 1928, the Cookshire Cemetery Association was reorganized and John French became a member of the Board of Trustees, marking the beginning of his more than 40 years of involvement with the cemetery:

> A meeting of the lot-owners and those interested in the Cookshire Cemetery was held in the basement of Victoria Hall on Monday evening, April 23rd, about forty-five being present. The object of the meeting was to consider the reorganization of the Cemetery Company; to change the name of the cemetery; to appoint a board of trustees and to discuss and adopt, if approved, the new by-laws submitted for the consideration of the meeting. It was decided to change the name "Cookshire Union Cemetery" to "The Cookshire Cemetery Association." The names of Messrs. J. E. Drennan, O. A. Osgood, L. G. Roy, John French and J. W. Robinson and Mrs. A. W. Pratt and Mrs. J. A. Frasier were submitted and by the unanimous vote of the meeting, they were elected a board of trustees . . . (*Sherbrooke Daily Record*, Apr. 27, 1928)

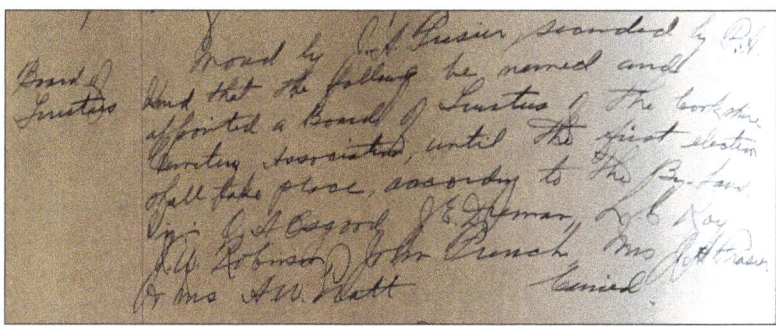

Cookshire Cemetery Association minutes re Board of Trustees, Apr. 23, 1928 (courtesy of Jack Garneau)

The charnel house

In 1936, the Cookshire Cemetery Association received a proposal from John French's brother, Charles Daniel French, to build a "charnel house" (i.e., a building or vault in which corpses or bones are piled) on the cemetery grounds. The French brothers had just completed the building of a new bridge across the Eaton River in Cookshire, and offered to build the vault gratis using the leftover materials from the bridge construction. After obtaining the concurrence of the Roman Catholics, the Association passed a motion to proceed with the project and then formalized the very unusual specifications for the structure. Extracts from meeting minutes follow:

Dearly beloved

That, whereas this Association has learned of the very kind and generous offer made to this Association by Mr. Charles D. French of Cookshire and Montreal, that is to erect a vault in our Cemetery (in conjunction with one for the use of the Roman Catholic Cemetery at the same time) be it resolved that the Cookshire Cemetery Association hereby accept this very munificent gift made by Mr. French and further [that] this Cookshire Cemetery Association hereby agrees to become responsible for the maintenance and up-keep of their one-half of said vault for all time. (Cookshire Cemetery Association meeting minutes, Aug. 27, 1936, courtesy of Jack Garneau)

Cookshire Cemetery vault (photo by author)

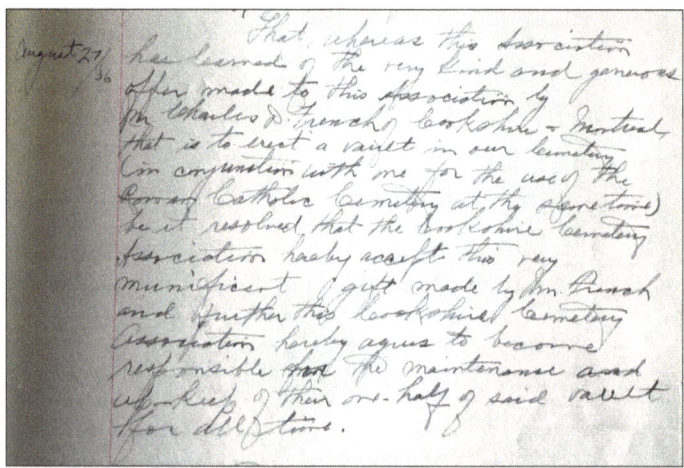

Cookshire Cemetery Association minutes re donation of vault, Aug. 27, 1936 (courtesy of Jack Garneau)

It is a practical and laudable action of Mr. French, and we have no objections for its realization. In order to maintain the good understanding that has always existed between the Catholics and Protestants of Cookshire, we believe that we must add what follows:

"1" That the construction of this charnel house, stands, by no means, in the way to any rights at all, acquired now or later by the Catholics

"2" That this charnel house has two entries, one for the Catholics and one for the Protestants, that it shall have an inside partition of least, of wood, to separate the part reserved to the Catholics from the part for the Protestants. (Cookshire Cemetery Association meeting minutes, Aug. 15, 1936, courtesy of Jack Garneau)

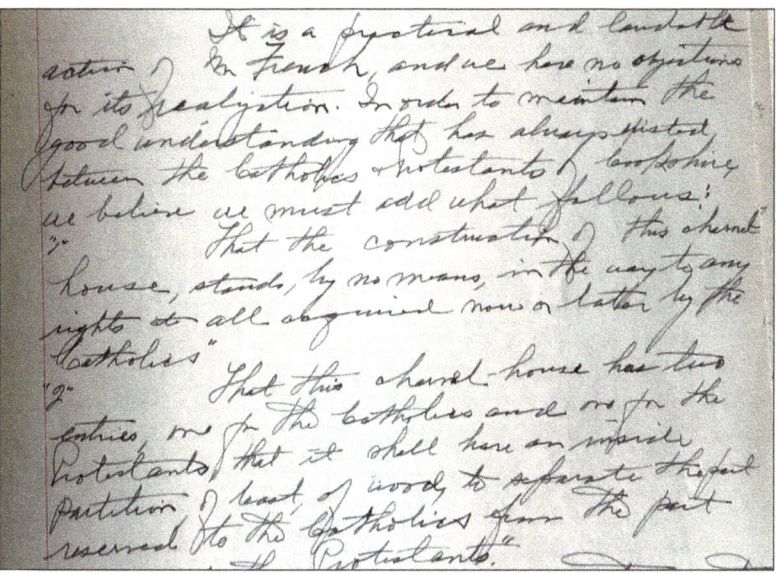

Cookshire Cemetery Association minutes re Roman Catholic concurrence, Aug. 15, 1936 (courtesy of Jack Garneau)

Half of the charnel-house will be on the Catholic side of the Cemetery, with inside partition dividing the two halves, also a door independent of the Protestants' part and opening towards the Catholic grave-yard. (Cookshire Cemetery Association minutes, Sep. 7, 1936, courtesy of Jack Garneau)

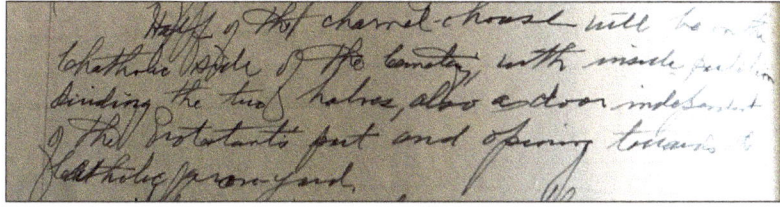

Cookshire Cemetery Association meeting minutes re charnel house specifications, Sep. 7, 1936 (courtesy of Jack Garneau)

Maintenance mission and memories

Cookshire Cemetery fence and grounds (photo by author)

In 1959, John French became president of the Cookshire Cemetery Association – a post that he held for almost the rest of his life. During his tenure a number of important improvements were made, including the installation of a new fence and gates. As well, he made it his personal mission to see that the cemetery grounds were meticulously maintained. Among the people he hired to that end was my brother Warren, who recalls his duties and his perspectives on working in such special surroundings.

> Often my friend Gilles Demers and I would cut the grass among the hundreds of tombstones in Cookshire Cemetery, as John French was the president of the Cookshire Cemetery Association. Late summer and early autumn, we used simple manual, double-edged serrated weed whippers to "couper les jaunes," as John French called this technique that didn't use gasoline and thus saved money. (The "jaunes" were yellow weeds known as "crépis des toits," a kind of hawks-beard.) (Warren Fraser)

"crépis des toits" weed (repertoirequebecnature.com)

Years before I first worked at the cemetery, my brother-in-law Dick Tracy would comment matter-of-factly that "people are dying to get in there" every time he drove us young Frasers for short rides, as we passed a cemetery. In 1967, when I first helped cut the grass around the gravestones, I would conjure up those long-ago words. However, I realized that those poor souls beneath me would never criticize my grass mowing skills, but my dear godfather might. There were times of distraction, when I would read many of the words on the stones, always hoping not to see my own name and discover that I had passed on! The gravestones told stories – in my mind – of the old and the young and the newborns, who had all died. "What had their lives been like?" and "Why did so many leave this earth at such young ages?" I silently wondered. During the two summers I worked at the cemetery, there were numerous instances of grave subsidence, so I had to tread gingerly with the lawnmower around the spongy depressions in front of those tombstones. I often feared that I might end up atop a skeleton. Should I be interred at the Cookshire Cemetery one day, I would imagine that I'd eventually be pushing up "les jaunes" instead of daisies. (Warren Fraser)

Not only was John French interested in the cemetery's maintenance and upkeep, he was fascinated by it as a place. John seemed undaunted by death. In his final years of life, he even seemed to look forward to the day when he would be deposited there. Family members recall incidents that reflect this attitude.

After attending the burial of a friend, Uncle John would say "Well, we planted John Smith today." (John French Wickenden)

At Aunt Ellen's funeral visitation, I remember Uncle John saying "Doesn't she look nice?" She was wearing her glasses! (Martha Wickenden MacKellar)

I recall Mom reporting, after stopping in to visit John and Dorothy, that John would comment "I'll soon be up on the hill." He could not have anticipated that Dorothy would lead the way. (Jim Fraser)

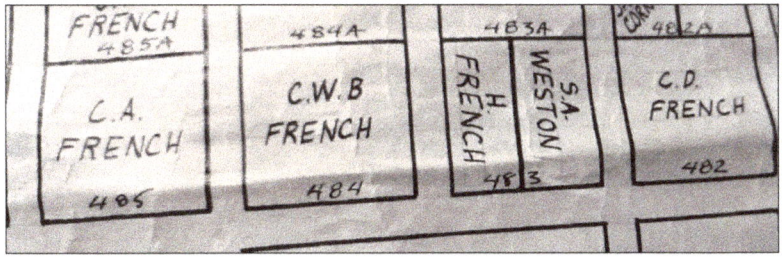

Map of French plots in Cookshire Cemetery (courtesy of Malcolm Learned)

No more room

When the cemetery was established, large plots were purchased by individual Cookshire families, including the Frenches. As years passed by and generations passed on, some of the plots became full. Such was the case for the Frenches, as noted by grandnephew Roger on a visit to the cemetery in 1970:

We took in a visit to the Cemetery and found Uncle John's grave alongside that of Aunt Dorothy in the MacLeod section rather than among the French "clan," perhaps a small and lasting indication as to how much Dorothy and her family had meant to him. (Roger Lancey)

Even though there was no more room for him in the Cookshire Cemetery's French family enclave, it didn't seem to bother John in the least, as illustrated by the following delightful anecdote from his grandniece Mary:

Mum [Jocelyn Wickenden Watson] had a story of Uncle John that I have delighted in retelling many times. As the family plot in the Cookshire Cemetery was full before he died, he was told he couldn't be buried there when his time came, which meant he'd have to be buried elsewhere in the cemetery. Asked whether he minded, he replied (and I paraphrase), "I don't mind at all; if I want to visit one of my relatives, I'll just get up and mosey over, like I always do." I always pause to say hello to him and have a quick chat when I visit the cemetery (for the record, he never talks back). From that tale alone, though, he sounds like someone I would have liked immensely. (Mary Watson)

"Just stopping by to say HELLO!" (sketch by James Harvey)

To John and Dorothy: May you rest in eternal peace "up on the hill."

Epilogue

Inscription on back of Uncle John photo by Jocelyn Wickenden Watson (courtesy of Mary Watson)

Perhaps, after reading this book, you may wonder why I chose "Dearly beloved" for the title.

Was it because John French and Dorothy MacLeod were dearly beloved by their respective families? Yes, partly. From everything I have learned from family members, they were dearly loved. But that was not the main reason.

Or was it because this couple dearly loved each other? Again, yes, but not entirely. From all external appearances, John and Dorothy absolutely adored each other. However, that was not the principal motivation.

Still yet, was it because of the high esteem in which they were held by members of the Cookshire community and the surrounding area? Indeed, John and Dorothy were greatly respected and much loved by all who knew them. Nonetheless, this fact was not the main impetus for the choice of a title.

Opening words of Anglican Church baptismal service (Book of Common Prayer, 1918)

Then what was it? As mentioned in the Preface, and elaborated in Chapter 10, John and Dorothy French were my godparents. In the Anglican Church of Canada's Book of Common Prayer, the baptismal service begins with the words "Dearly beloved . . ."

In addition, you may have asked why each chapter began with a literary quotation. The reason is very straightforward. It is in tribute to Dorothy's well-known and much appreciated recitations of poetry and prose. Also, it is in recognition of the belletristic proclivities demonstrated by so many members of later generations of the French family.

Winston

As a tribute to John and Dorothy's love of young people, a portion of the proceeds from the sale of this book will be used to establish an annual special prize at Cookshire Fair for the best essay of 500 to 1000 words on any subject by a Compton County student under the age of 17. The prize will be known as "The John and Dorothy French Memorial Youth Literary Prize."

Dearly beloved

Appendix
Ancestral Obituaries Scrapbook

This appendix contains a collection of obituaries, death notices and gravestone photos for John and Dorothy French, their parents and their siblings.

- John Wellington French
- Dorothy Isabella MacLeod French
- Charles Ward Bailey French (John's father)
- Maria A. Bailey (John's stepmother)
- Catherine "Kate" MacIver (John's mother)
- John F. McLeod (Dorothy's father)
- Catherine MacLeod (Dorothy's mother)
- Persis "Pertie" French (John's half-sister)
- Ellen Bailey French (John's half-sister)
- Herbert Arthur French (John's half-brother)
- Charles Daniel French (John's brother)
- Eva Mary MacLeod Shirreffs (Dorothy's sister)
- Horace Roderick French (John's brother)
- Charlotte Muriel Mabel "Lottie" French Mackenzie (John's sister)
- Annie Eliza Catherine French Wickenden (John's sister)

Dearly beloved

John Wellington French

J. W. FRENCH of Cookshire

After a number of years of impaired health, John Wellington French died very suddenly at his home on Nov. 8, 1970, at the age of 82 years.

Mr. French was born in Scotstown, Oct. 22, 1888. He was the son of the late Charles Ward Bailey French and his wife, Catherine MacIver (Scotch). His family, on his paternal side, came from Connecticut in 1797, and settled in Compton County. His maternal grandparents came from Scotland, and settled in Gould, Que.

Mr. French received his education at the Scotstown and Cookshire High Schools.

On March 12, 1935, he married Dorothy Isabella MacLeod, of Cookshire, daughter of the late Mr. and Mrs. John MacLeod. The ceremony was performed at the home of Mrs. French's brother-in-law and sister, Mr. and Mrs. H. W. Shirreffs, in Bronxville, N.Y., with Rev. Johnston officiating. There were no children from this marriage, but they were both very fond of children, and several nieces and nephews enjoyed visiting at their home, and were very happy in their company.

Mr. French was a retired contractor, he was a councillor from 1925-1935, a member of the school board from 1935-1940 and also a Mason. He was elected as a member of the Quebec Legislative Assembly at a by-election on Sept. 15, 1954, for the Union Nationale Government, and completed the term of office for his brother, the late C.D. French, until June 1956.

He was keenly interested in the welfare of the citizens, not only of Cookshire, but of the whole county, and gave unstintingly of his time, talents and money to help improve of the Cookshire Cemetery was greatly appreciated by all who knew him, and is a fine monument to his efforts.

Mrs. French predeceased her husband on May 23, 1970, and the past six months he has sadly missed her bright smile and devoted companionship.

The remains rested at French's Funeral Parlor in Cookshire until Nov. 10, 1970, and the funeral service was held in St. Peter's Anglican Church in Cookshire at 2 p.m., with Rev. Alan Fairbairn officiating, assisted by the Rev. Father Querion, of Martinville, who spoke in French as there were many French people in attendance to show their last respects to one of their benefactors. The choir led in the singing of The Lord's My Shepherd, Unto the Hills, and Peace, Perfect Peace as a recessional, with Mrs. George Gill at the console. The United Church Choir was also represented in the choir.

The bearers were J. F. Wickenden, W. F. Buckle, Don French, J. K. Watson, Malcolm Fraser, Paul St. Laurent. The interment was in the Cookshire Protestant Cemetery.

Those left to mourn his passing are Horace French (brother) of Wetaskiwin, Alta., Mrs. M. K. Mackenzie (sister Lottie) of Cookshire, Mrs. J. F. Wickenden, (sister Annie) of Three Rivers, Que., Mrs. H. W. Shirriffs, (sister-in-law) of Bronxville, N. Y., several nieces, nephews and and other relatives and friends.

John W. French obituary (*Sherbrooke Daily Record*, Dec. 9, 1970)

Dorothy Isabella MacLeod French

MRS. DOROTHY ISABELLA FRENCH OF COOKSHIRE

COOKSHIRE — The relatives and friends of the late Mrs. Dorothy Isabella French were shocked to hear of her sudden death at the Hotel Dieu Hospital in Sherbrooke on Saturday, May 23, 1970, at the age of 79 years.

Mrs. French was born in Gould on May 11, 1891, the daughter of the late John F. MacLeod, and his wife, Catherine MacLeod.

When quite young, she and her family moved to Bury, where she attended the High School. She also attended Macdonald College where she received her teacher's diploma, and taught in Aberdeen School in Montreal for a few years. She later worked in the office of Belding Corticelli in Montreal, but came to Cookshire to care for her mother in 1928, following her father's death.

While living in Bury, she attended the old Methodist Church, and taught in the Sunday School. After coming to Cookshire she was equally interested in church work, and attended the United and Anglican churches. She was keenly interested in the Women's Institute, and was made a Life Member of that society. She had also been a member of Unity Chapter No. 3, O.E.S. She liked to recite poetry, and many of the town's societies enjoyed her selections.

On March 12, 1935, she was married to John W. French, of Cookshire; the marriage ceremony was held at the home of her brother-in-law and sister, Mr. and Mrs. H. W. Shirreffs, in Bronxville, New York, with the Rev. Johnston officiating.

The remains rested at French's Funeral Parlor in Cookshire until Tuesday, May 26th, and the funeral service was held in St. Peter's Anglican Church, Cookshire, at 2 p.m., with the Rev. Alan Fairbairn, of Cookshire, the Rev. Carl Gustafson, of Lennoxville, and the Rev. Father Quirion, of Martinville, officiating.

The bearers were Messrs. H. A. Plow, Brian McDermott, Paul St. Laurent, James French, Lionel Pope and Malcolm Fraser.

The interment was in the Cookshire Protestant Cemetery.

Those left to mourn her passing are her husband, John W. French, of Cookshire, her sister Eva, (Mrs. H. W. Shirreffs) of Bronxville, N.Y., a number of nieces, nephews and other relatives, and her numerous friends.

Dorothy French obituary (*Sherbrooke Daily Record*, June 26, 1970)

Charles Ward Bailey French (John's father)

> **FEU C. W. B. FRENCH**
>
> (Du correspondant régulier de LA PRESSE)
> Sherbrooke, 18 — C. W. B. French, populaire hôtellier de Scotstown est décédé à sa demeure, à la suite d'une maladie de quelques jours seulement. Le défunt était âgé de 59 ans, et comptait une foule d'amis qui regretteront vivement sa fin prématurée. Les funérailles ont eu lieu hier après-midi.

Charles W. B. French death notice (*La Presse*, May 18, 1905)

Charles W. B. French gravestone, Cookshire Cemetery (photo by author)

Scotstown.

OBITUARY.—Your correspondent has a sad duty to perform this week in recording the death of Mrs. Charles W. B. French of the Scotstown Hotel, who died on Monday morning last. Her numerous good qualities endeared her to all who had the privilege of her acquaintance, without exception. Her happy and kindly countenance will be greatly missed in our community here. Mr. French has lost a dutiful wife, and his three small children—the youngest not yet a month old—have been deprived of a fond and loving mother. Mrs. French was the daughter of C. A. Baily, Esq., Cookshire. The bereaved ones have the deepest sympathy of a large circle of friends and acquaintances in their affliction. The funeral on Wednesday to Cookshire was numerously attended by friends from Scotstown, Cookshire and surrounding localities.

Obituary of Maria Bailey, Charles W. B. French's first wife (*Weekly Examiner*, Feb. 6, 1880)

Dearly beloved

Catherine "Kate" MacIver (John's mother)

MRS. C. W. B. FRENCH, COOKSHIRE.

Cookshire, December 26. — The community was saddened by the sudden passing on Friday morning, December 15th, of Mrs. Catherine MacIver French, widow of the late Charles W. B. French, formerly of Scotstown, Que.

Mrs. French was born at Red Mountain, Que., in 1857 and was married in February, 1883, to her late husband who predeceased her in 1905. They resided in Scotstown. Following Mr. French's death, the deceased moved with her two daughters to Humboldt, Minn., where she resided for four year, then came to Cookshire and has since made her home with her son, Mr. John W. French.

Her unselfish and kindly manner and generous hospitality endeared her to a large circle of friends, whose heartfelt sympathy is extended to the bereaved family in their irreparable loss.

The funeral took place on Tuesday December 19th. Prayers were said at the late residence by Rev. E. M. Tulk, followed by a simple but beautifully impressive service at St. Peter's Church. The rector was assisted by Rev. R W. Carr, pastor of Trinity United Church, who read the lesson. Mr. Tulk spoke words of comfort to the sorrowing family, taking as his theme, "The Love of God," to which, he said, a mother's love comes nearest. He also referred to her many acts of kindness to others outside the family circle, likening her deeds to those of Deborah of old. The choir led the singing of three favorite hymns, "Jesus, Saviour, Pilot Me," "There Is No Night in Heaven" and "Now the Laborer's Task is O'er."

The floral tributes were numerous and very beautiful. Interment took place in the family lot in Cookshire Cemetery.

Mrs. French leaves to mourn her loss, three sons, Charles D., of Westmount, John W., of Cookshire, and Horace R., of Wetaskiwin, Alta.; two daughters, Mrs. Malcolm K. MacKenzie, of Montreal West, and Mrs. John F. Wickenden, of Three Rivers; and two step-daughters, the Misses Persis and Ellen French, of Cookshire; all of whom were present at the funeral with the exception of Miss Persis who is ill. There are also two sisters and five brothers who reside in the west, as well as fifteen grandchildren. Two daughters predeceased their mother before the death of their father.

Obituary of Catherine "Kate" MacIver (*Sherbrooke Daily Record*, Dec. 26, 1933)

John F. McLeod (Dorothy's father)

John F. MacLeod gravestone, Cookshire Cemetery (photo by author)

MR. JOHN F. MacLEOD, COOKSHIRE.

COOKSHIRE, Que., May 16.— There passed away at his late residence on March 31st, Mr. John Frazier MacLeod, son of the late John and Dorothy MacLeod, of Gould, Que., where he was born, September 1st, 1849.

The funeral service was held at two p.m. on Sunday, April 1st. Rev. C. C. James of the United Church officiating. Rev. A. W. Buckland, rector of St. Peter's Church, and grand chaplain of St. Francis District, A.F. and A.M., conducted the Masonic service, assisted by the officers and members of Friendship Lodge. The interment took place at Cookshire cemetery.

The bearers were Messrs. K. McCaskell, E. Morrison and R. Morrison, of Keith, and Dr. J. A. Butler and Misses A. W. Pratt and J. French, of Cookshire.

The beautiful floral tributes came from relatives and friends from Keith, Bury, Cookshire, Sherbrooke, Montreal, Port Chester and New York City all bringing comfort to the bereaved family and testifying to the high esteem in which the deceased was held.

Mr. MacLeod had been in business in Bury for twenty-three years, coming to reside in Cookshire seven years ago, when he retired from active life. He was a member of Friendship Lodge, A.F. and A.M., of Cookshire, since 1881 and was also a Fenian Raid veteran. He participated in the celebration here in 1867 of the first Dominion Day and was one of the four veterans who were in the procession during the Jubilee celebrations last year.

The deceased had been in failing health for some time but was able to be about until he was suddenly stricken on Wednesday afternoon, March 28th. He passed away early the following morning, without regaining consciousness.

Besides his wife, formerly Catharine MacLeod, of Keith, the deceased is survived by two daughters, Mrs. H. W. Shirreffs, of New York City, and Miss Dorothy MacLeod; one granddaughter, Miss Dorothy E. MacL. Shirreffs, and many nieces and nephews.

The relatives from out of town who attended the funeral were Mr. and Mrs. F. G. H. MacLeod and Mr. and Mrs. E. Morrison, of Keith; Mrs. J. MacLeod, of Scotstown, and Mr. H. W. Shirreffs, of New York City. Mrs. H. W. Shirreffs was unable to be present owing to illness.

Obituary of John F. MacLeod (*Sherbrooke Daily Record*, May 16, 1928)

Dearly beloved

Catherine MacLeod (Dorothy's mother)

FUNERAL OF MRS. J. F. MacLEOD

Cookshire, June 20.—The funeral of Mrs. Catherine MacLeod, widow of the late John Frazier MacLeod, was held at the residence on Sunday, May 28. The service was conducted by Rev. E. M. Wilson, of Sawyerville. The choir of Trinity United Church sang the hymn, "Forever With the Lord," and Mr. A. W. Pratt sang "Sleep On, Beloved, Sleep and Take Thy Rest."

Mrs. MacLeod leaves to mourn her loss, daughters, Mrs. H. W. Shirreffs, of Bronxville, N.Y., and Miss Dorothy I. MacLeod, of Cookshire; Miss Dorothy E. Shirreffs, granddaughter; Mr. Frank G. H. MacLeod, of Keith, a nephew; Mr. Lyman Armitage, of Coaticook, a great nephew; Mrs. Norman MacDonald and Miss Margaret Buchanan, of North Hill, nieces; Mrs. Powers and Mr. Alex MacKay, of North Hill, Mrs. Norman MacLeod and Mr. and Mrs. John Bailey, of Lake Megantic, and Mrs. E. Morrison, of Keith, cousins.

Among those from out of town who attended the funeral were: Mr. and Mrs. Wm. McCaskill, Mr. and Mrs. Colin Morrison, Mrs. A. Buchanan, Mrs. W. Buchanan and Mr. K. MacLeod, all of Keith; Mr. and Mrs. E. A. Stokes, Miss Edythe Stokes, Mr. A. Pehlemann, Miss E. Pehelmann, Mrs. A. D. MacLeod, Mr. and Mrs. J. S. Saunders and Mr. and Mrs. M. T. Stokes, of Bury; Mr. P. H. Armitage and Miss Carrie Armitage, of Coaticook; Mr. and Mrs. M. V. Long, Mr. and Mrs. Miller Hall, Miss H. Henderson, Miss C. Hyndman, Mr. Angus MacIver, Mrs. Holgate, Miss M. MacIver and Mr. and Mrs. F. E. Kerridge, all of Sherbrooke.

Catherine MacLeod obituary (*Sherbrooke Daily Record*, June 22, 1933)

Persis "Pertie" French (John's half-sister)

Ellen French and Pertie French gravestone, Cookshire Cemetery (photo by Leslie Nutbrown)

Dearly beloved

Ellen Bailey French (John's half-sister)

MISS ELLEN FRENCH, OF COOKSHIRE

COOKSHIRE — On June 25, 1964, Miss Ellen Bailey French died in the Sherbrooke Hospital, after a brief illness.

Miss French, the second daughter of Charles W. B. French and Maria Augusta Bailey, was born May 19, 1878, in Scotstown, where she spent her early years.

Following her father's death in 1905, she came to live in Cookshire, where she graduated from the Academy and then attended Normal School in Montreal. After teaching for a few years, she returned to Cookshire to live with her aunts, the Misses Abbie and Ann Bailey and her invalid sister, Pertie. After their deaths, she remained in Cookshire.

She was a faithful member of St. Peter's Church, was active in the Guild and a supporter of all worthy causes.

Left to mourn are two brothers, John, of Cookshire, and Horace, of Wetaskiwin, Alta.; and two sisters, Lottie, Mrs. M. K. MacKenzie, of Montreal West and Annie, Mrs. J. F. Wickenden, of Three Rivers, and many other relatives.

On June 30, prayers were conducted at her home by Rev. Morley Thomas, followed by the funeral service in St. Peter's Church, with Mr. Thomas officiating. The choir, with Mrs. George Gill as organist, led in the singing of two favorite hymns, Unto the Hills and Abide with Me.

The bearers were John McDonald, Malcolm Fraser, Darrell Bellam, Everiste Rousseau, Malcolm McVetty and Lionel Pope. Interment was in Cookshire Cemetery.

Mourners included Mr. and Mrs. John French, Mr. and Mrs. M. K. MacKenzie, Mr. and Mrs. J. F. Wickenden, Sr., Mr. and Mrs. C. Don French, Mrs. Sterling Whiteway, Mrs. Bruce Ferguson, Miss Jean Wickenden, Mrs. J. C. McKellar, Mr. and Mrs. J. F. Wickenden, Jr., Mrs. R. J. Stevenson and Mrs. E. A. Bailey.

Numerous friends from Scotstown, Bury, Sherbrooke and the surrounding district attended.

Ellen French obituary (*Sherbrooke Daily Record*, July 15, 1964)

Herbert Arthur French (John's half-brother)

FATAL ACCIDENT AT ACTONVALE

CIRCUMSTANCES OF DEATH OF HERBERT FRENCH, SON OF LATE C.W.B. FRENCH, FORMERLY OF SCOTSTOWN.

Mr. Herbert A. French of Montreal, formerly of Scotstown and son of the late C. W. B. French of that town was accidentally killed at Actonvale, Que., September 13th. He had been in the employ of the Grand Trunk Railway as trainman for several years between Island Pond and Montreal. The accident occurred last Wednesday evening while on duty at Actonvale.

His remains were brought to Cookshire for burial. The deceased leaves to mourn his loss a wife and three small children as well as a large number of relatives and friends.

Herbert French accident death notice (*Sherbrooke Daily Record*, Sep. 19, 1916)

Herbert, Pertie and Ellen French gravestone, Cookshire Cemetery (courtesy of Roger Lancey)

Charles Daniel French (John's brother)

Hon. C. D. French, Mines Minister, Dies

The Eastern Townships, and especially the County of Compton, today mourn the passing of Hon. Charles Daniel French, Minister of Mines in the Provincial Government and Member of the Legislative Assembly for Compton County, whose death occurred at his home in Montreal last night following an illness of almost ten months duration. He was in his 71st year.

Although residing in Montreal for many years, Mr. French kept a close interest in his native county and spent much of his time at his country home in Cookshire where he bred prize Belgian horses and Ayrshire and Hereford cattle.

The funeral service will be held at St. Peter's Church in Cookshire on Friday afternoon at 2 p.m. following a service to be held in Dominion Douglas Church, Montreal, at 2 p.m., Thursday. Interment will be in Cookshire Cemetery.

Mr. French was born at Scotstown, Que., in 1884, a member of an old English and Scottish family that first settled in Compton County in 1790 and he belonged to the fourth generation born in the district.

He was first elected to the Quebec legislature for Compton riding at a by-election in July, 1946. Following his re-election in the 1948 provincial general election he was appointed Mines minister in Premier Duplessis' Union Nationale government.

He is survived by his widow, a son, Donald, a daughter, Enid, and three grandchildren, the children of Donald, Miss Enid, a teacher, flew from Moncton, N.B. to the bedside of her father. Other survivors include two brothers, Horace, Wetaskiwin, Alta., and John, Cookshire, Que.; and three sisters, Mrs. S. J. Wickenden, Three Rivers, Que., Miss Ellen French, Cookshire, and Mrs. Malcolm McKenzie, Montreal.

Mr. French became seriously ill last year and was unable to attend the recent session of the legislature.

A newcomer to politics when first elected, he stepped into a cabinet post made vacant a few months earlier by the death of the late Mines Minister Jonathan Robinson.

Rugged-looking but soft spoken, he was the only Protestant English-speaking member of the Quebec cabinet. He was held in high esteem by politicians on both sides of the legislature.

Although he spoke French with some difficulty, he came through in two general elections to win handily over French-speaking opponents in his constituency, where the voters are about evenly divided between English-speaking and French-speaking groups.

He took over the mines portfolio at a time when Quebec's mining development was in full swing.

It was during his term that explorations were pushed ahead in northwestern Quebec and in the Chibougamau area.

His term also coincided with the construction of a 360-mile railroad from Sept Iles to Knob Lake in the heart of Ungava where iron ore mining operations are scheduled to get under way this summer.

Between 1919 and his entry into politics in 1946 he was president of Kennedy Construction Company of Montreal.

The death of Mr. French creates the first vacancy in the Quebec legislative assembly since 1952. Standing now is Union Nationale 67, Liberals 23, independent one, vacant one.

HON. C. D. FRENCH

C.D. French death notice (*Sherbrooke Daily Record*, May 4, 1954)

C. D. French and Emily Macaulay gravestone, Cookshire Cemetery (photo by Leslie Nutbrown)

Eva Mary MacLeod Shirreffs (Dorothy's sister)

Eva M. Shirreffs

Eva M. Shirreffs, 95, of Foulk Manor North, 1212 Foulk Road, formerly of Bronxville, N.Y., died Tuesday at the retirement home of pneumonia.

Mrs. Shirreffs was a homemaker. She was a member of West Center Congregational Church, Bronxville. She was a supporter of Teen Challenge at the Walter Hoving Home, Garrison, N.Y.

Her husband, Harry W., died in 1950. She is survived by two granddaughters, Kathryn L. Kressman and Nancy J. Kressman, both of New Castle.

Services will be Thursday at 7:30 p.m. in the Chandler Funeral Home, 2506 Concord Pike, Sharpley. Burial will be in Cookshire Cemetery, Cookshire, Quebec, Canada. There will be no viewing.

Eva MacLeod Shirreffs obituary (*The Morning News*, Wilmington Del., May 16, 1984)

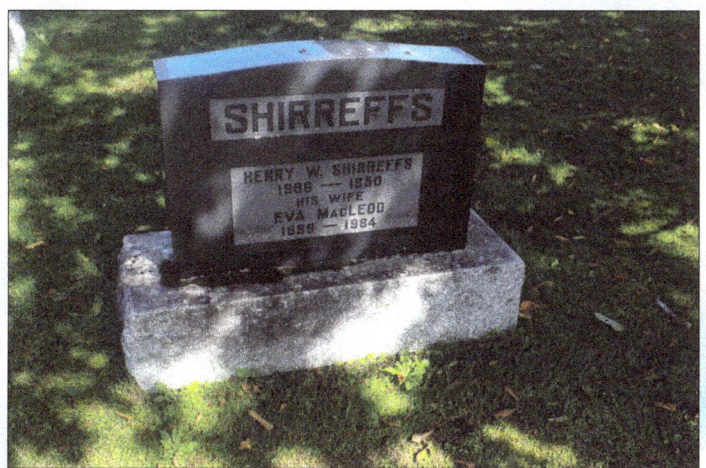

Eva and Harry Shirreffs gravestone, Cookshire Cemetery (photo by author)

Dearly beloved

Horace Roderick French (John's brother)

H.R. FRENCH
formerly of Scotstown

A well known and respected businessman of this community for over sixty years, Horace R. "Frenchie" French passed away in Wetaskiwin on Saturday, May 25. He was 84 years of age.

Mr. French maintained a keen interest in business and community affairs throughout his many years here. Up until February of 1973 he spent each and every day in his jewellery store repairing watches, selling items of jewellery, discussing local and national topics of the day or spinning tales about his friends and experiences of an earlier time. He possessed a rare sense of humor and was not above playing a practical joke on any of his friends who were the least bit unwary. These pranks were of a harmless nature, but never failed to bring a moment of mirth even to the "victim."

Among his many acquaintances and associates there were those who also knew "tricks of the trade" when it came to practical jokes, and perhaps those occurrences which "Frenchie" enjoyed most were those where he was the victim.

"Frenchie" was born in Scotstown, Quebec, March 10, 1890, where he received his education and began his lifetime work in the repair and jewellery trade.

On November 8, 1909 Mr. French began work in the jewellery store of C. C. Bailey, Wetaskiwin. He came to Mr. Bailey on the recommendation of a customer for the excellent repair work on a pipe.

After serving in the Royal Flying Corps as a pilot in the First World War, "Frenchie" returned and purchased the jewellery store from Mr. Thomas in 1921.

"Frenchie" was married to Annie Angus in 1920 and to this union was born two sons, Charles Roderick and Malcolm Angus.

He was also a practising optometrist for many years but relinquished this portion of the business to his son Rod in 1950. He and his son Mac were in partnership in the jewellery business and the store is still in the original location.

"Frenchie" served on the city council from 1928 - 1932. He was a charter member of the Wetaskiwin Kiwanis Club and was presented with the Kiwanis Legion of Honor Award on April 20, 1974 when the Club celebrated its 50th anniversary. He had served as second president of the club. He was also a member of the Masonic Lodge.

Sports were a main interest in his life and he played both baseball and hockey on the Wetaskiwin teams in the early days. He was also an ardent hunter and a keen fisherman.

In 1962 "Frenchie" received the Citizen of the Year Award from the Chamber of Commerce and Agriculture. He participated in the official opening of the Wetaskiwin Municipal Airport on May 5, 1974 by cutting the ribbon.

He is survived by his loving wife, two sons, Rod and Mac of Wetaskiwin; four grandchildren; two sisters Mrs. Lottie MacKenzie and Mrs. Annie Wickenden in Quebec.

Funeral services was held May 29 at 2:00 p.m. in the Anglican Church with Rev. Winchester officiating and interment in the Wetaskiwin Cemetery.

Baker Chapel in charge of all arrangements.

He went by many names 'F.R.', 'Frenchy', 'Mr. French', and to a chosen few 'Dad', but somehow they all very aptly suited the individual to whom they applied. And he wore every one of them well. These were the name tags that many friends and acquaintances used when they talked about him in his absence.

One form of address I for one never heard was "Old Man French." But then this is not too surprising because Horace French never reached the stage of being an old man. True, he had spent many a day at this business of living and after most people reach the age of 80 years they are described as being old, long in the tooth and any number of similar semi-derogatory terms which tends to describe any one who is not really "with it anymore".

For those people who had the good fortune to cross paths with 'Frenchy', they will know what I mean when I say that there was a puckish individual, one who had zest for life and was concerned about those he came in contact with. He was quick to perceive what was right with the world, quick to recognize what needed changing, and equally quick to condemn those areas which were wrong and beyond changing. What's more he didn't mince words. He expressed his opinion and whether or not you agreed didn't alter that opinion. It was his, and as far as he was concerned you were entitled to yours, but he was not about to be swayed for the sake of convenience of the moment.

As mentioned above 'Frenchy' was not one to dwell in the past. Sure he enjoyed talking about experiences and friends from an earlier day, but he always seemed to turn the conversation back to the present day and what was going on now. The present time was his big interest. Talk about the "now" generation back in the early 1900's and through the years just didn't keep up with the times, but was ahead of them.

It's a time of sadness when one such as this leaves our midst. On the other hand it is not the end of the world. People such as H.R. 'Frenchy' French realized that life wouldn't stop with their passing — they built and lived and planned in a manner that this would not be the case.

Horace French obituary (*Sherbrooke Daily Record*, July 8, 1974)

Charlotte Muriel Mabel "Lottie" French Mackenzie (John's sister)

LOTTIE MacKENZIE of Cookshire

Mrs. Lottie MacKenzie passed away in the Sherbrooke Hospital on Saturday, April 26, 1980, after a short illness, in her 89th year.

Mrs. MacKenzie, nee Lottie Muriel Mabel French was born on July 23, 1891, at Scotstown, daughter of the late C.W.B. French and his late wife, Catherine MacIver French.

She received part of her education at the Cookshire Academy. The family moved to Winnipeg, where she finished her education, obtaining a teacher's diploma from the Winnipeg Collegiate Institute, and taught at Swan River for a number of years.

She met her husband-to-be, Malcolm Kenneth MacKenzie, of Plaister Mines, N.S., in Winnipeg, and they were married on August 28, 1918, in St. Peter's Church, Cookshire, and spent most of their married life in Montreal West, where she was active in the Women's Club.

After her husband retired from work in the Dominion Bridge Company, they came to live in Cookshire in 1965. Mr. MacKenzie predeceased her on May 29, 1972, and the remains were placed in the Cookshire Cemetery in the family plot.

Mrs. MacKenzie was also predeceased by an infant son, Rodney French, in 1923, and her daughter, Mary, in 1958, also by her brothers, the Honorable C.D. French, of Westmount and Cookshire, John W. French, M.L.A., of Cookshire, Horace French, of Wetaskewin, Alta., and her sisters Ellen and Pertie French of Cookshire.

Her remains rested at the L.O. Cass and Son-Gordon Smith Funeral Home in Cookshire, where her many friends called to pay their respects to a very fine senior lady.

The service was held in St. Peter's Anglican Church, Cookshire, on Tuesday, April 29, at 3:30 p.m. with the Rev. H.A. Vallis officiating, and the organist, Mrs. Mary E. Heatherington providing appropriate funeral music.

The pall bearers were two grandsons, Ian Ferguson and William Gallert, a nephew, Donald French, and a young friend, Jean-Marc Demers.

Interment was in the Cookshire Cemetery beside her late husband in the French's family plot.

Those left to mourn her passing are her three daughters, Mrs. Margaret Buckle, Cookshire, Mrs. Ruth Whiteway, Dartmouth, N.S., Mrs. Rhona Ferguson, Montreal, her sister Annie, Mrs. J.F. Wickenden, of Westmount, formerly of Three Rivers, six grandchildren, Miss Leslie Buckle, Calgary, Alta., Ronald Buckle and his wife Lynn, of Vancouver, Malcolm Whiteway, Edmonton, Lorne Whiteway, Dartmouth, N.S., Ian Ferguson and his sister Mrs. William Gallert, of Montreal, a number of nieces, nephews and many friends.

Lottie French Mackenzie obituary (*The Record*, May 8, 1980)

Lottie French and Malcolm Mackenzie gravestone, Cookshire Cemetery (photo by Leslie Nutbrown)

Annie Eliza Catherine French Wickenden (John's sister)

WICKENDEN, Anne French. Peacefully at Pierrefonds Manor, Pierrefonds, Quebec on July 30, 1991 in her ninety-fourth year. Beloved wife of the late John F. Dear mother of Jean Mooney (McKillop), Stittsville, Ontario, Jocelyn Watson (Jim), Pointe Claire, Quebec, Martha MacKellar (Jim), Don Mills, Ontario, Harriet Taylor (Roy), Oakville, Ontario, Alice MacEwen (Peter), Morrisburg, Ontario and John (Bonnie), Bainsville, Ontario. Also survived by sixteen grandchildren and six great-grandchildren. Private funeral service was held in Trois Rivieres, Quebec followed by interment at Forest Hills Cemetery. Donations to the charity of your choice will be gratefully acknowledged.

Annie French Wickenden obituary (*The Gazette*, July 30, 1991)

John Wickenden and Annie French gravestone, Forest Hill Cemetery, Trois-Rivières (findagrave.com)

www.ingramcontent.com/pod-product-compliance
Lightning Source LLC
Chambersburg PA
CBHW040108120526
44589CB00040B/2808